VOID

Library of
Davidson College

Lilika Nakos

Twayne's World Authors Series

TWAS 677

Deborah Tannen and Lilika Nakos at Nakos' home in Halandri, outside Athens, 1976. Photograph by Harry Weinreb.

Lilika Nakos

By Deborah Tannen

Georgetown University

Twayne Publishers • Boston

889.3
N163 xt

Lilika Nakos

Deborah Tannen

Copyright © 1983 by G. K. Hall & Company
All Rights Reserved
Published by Twayne Publishers
A Division of G. K. Hall & Company
70 Lincoln Street
Boston, Massachusetts 02111

Printed on permanent/durable acid-free
paper and bound in The United States
of America.

Excerpts from the works of Lilika Nakos,
translated by Deborah Tannen, are
reprinted by permission of Aristeidis
Klados of Dorikos Press, Athens, Greece.

Library of Congress Cataloging in Publication Data

Tannen, Deborah.
   Lilika Nakos.

   (Twayne's world authors series ; TWAS 677)
      Bibliography: p. 180
      Includes index.
      1. Nakos, Lilika—Criticism and interpretation.
   I. Title. II. Series.
PA5610.N3Z88 1983   889'.332 [B]   82-15441
ISBN 0-8057-6524-7

85-0691

To Mimi and Naomi
my sisters
in every sense of the word

Contents

About the Author
Preface
Chronology

> *Chapter One*
> Restlessness and Commitment: Life and Times   1
>
> *Chapter Two*
> Loneliness and Hunger: Short Stories   25
>
> *Chapter Three*
> Cruel Fatherland: *The Deflowered One*   45
>
> *Chapter Four*
> The Holy Virgin in Hell: *The Lost*   59
>
> *Chapter Five*
> "Never Love a Man": *Nafsika*   80
>
> *Chapter Six*
> Comic Lament on a Rocky Coast: *Mrs. Doremi*   93
>
> *Chapter Seven*
> Return to Greek Roots: *Boetian Earth*   104
>
> *Chapter Eight*
> Political Bitterness and Personal Hope:
> *Toward a New Life*   126
>
> *Chapter Nine*
> Happily Ever After: *Ikarian Dreamers*   144
>
> *Chapter Ten*
> Conclusion   163

Notes and References   169
Selected Bibliography   180
Index   187

About the Author

Deborah Tannen is Assistant Professor of Linguistics at Georgetown University. She holds a Ph.D. and M.A. in linguistics from the University of California, Berkeley; an M.A. in English and General Literature from Wayne State University; and a B.A. in English Literature from Harpur College, the State University of New York at Binghamton.

In the field of literature, Dr. Tannen has published articles on the work of Lilika Nakos and other modern Greek women writers, as well as on the work of James Joyce and William Butler Yeats.

In the field of linguistics, Dr. Tannen's research has focused on the analysis of conversation; narrative; spoken and written discourse; and doctor/patient communication. In all these areas she has compared American English and modern Greek discourse.

In addition to numerous scholarly articles, Dr. Tannen is the author of *Conversational Style: Analyzing Talk Among Friends* (Norwood, N.J.: Ablex, 1983). She has edited four volumes of collected papers: *Spoken and Written Language: Exploring Orality and Literacy* (Norwood, N.J.: Ablex, 1982); *Georgetown University Round Table on Languages and Linguistics 1981, Analyzing Discourse: Text and Talk* (Washington, D.C.: Georgetown University Press, 1982); *Coherence in Spoken and Written Discourse* (Norwood, N.J.: Ablex); and *Functions of Silence* (in preparation), jointly edited with Muriel Saville-Troike.

Dr. Tannen has published original poems and short stories and has won prizes for both. She has received a Danforth Graduate Fellowship, a National Endowment for the Humanities Summer Stipend, and a Rockefeller Foundation Humanities Fellowship.

Preface

Lilika Nakos was one of the first women writers of modern Greek prose and for many years the only woman in Greek journalism. She was a member of the Generation of the Thirties, the group of writers who forged a modern novel in Greek. A study of Nakos's work is needed for an understanding of modern Greek literature. Moreover, it is needed to open the way for in-depth studies of women's contributions to modern Greek prose.

During the seven months I spent in Athens researching and writing the first draft of this book, I was a constant visitor at Nakos's homes in Halandri and Ekali, and I came to know her intimately. The deep friendship that grew between us then has continued through correspondence and regular visits and has been for me the most precious fruit of this labor.

Surprisingly, this friendship did not assist me in my critical task in the way I had anticipated. Nakos has always been impulsive, careless, even eccentric. For example, a friend of hers told of visiting Nakos as a young woman in Paris when she received an expensive silk dress as a gift from her father. Nakos pushed the dress into a lump and tossed it under the bed. This cavalier attitude extends to her work as well. She has kept no copies of her publications and no record of them. (When I managed, with great effort, to locate many of her early stories in old magazines and newspapers, I gave her copies of every one. By the time a publisher decided to reprint them in a collection, Nakos had misplaced them all.) When I apologized for the delay in the publication of this book, Nakos wrote to me, "If it comes out; if it doesn't come out—it's all the same!" This ingenuousness made Nakos's acquaintance precious to me, but it did not ease my critical task. She could direct me to almost no published stories or critical reviews.

LILIKA NAKOS

The Twayne format requires a chronology. Alas, in this regard Nakos seemed more anxious to confound than to enlighten me. "This woman lived outside of time!" she announced into my tape recorder. "Write that!" If I interrupted her account of events to pin her down to dates, she might cut short her narrative. She quickly grew impatient of questions: "Oh, you and your chronology! I don't remember dates!" She was displeased to learn that I was trying to establish chronology from other sources.

Despite this reluctance with regard to chronology, Nakos was selflessly giving of her time and spirit, talking openly about her thoughts and experiences, more and more as we knew each other better. She opened her heart and her life and became part of mine. Therefore, this book, in addition to assessing and analyzing her work, gives a subjective view of Nakos as a person and a personality. It could not be otherwise.

The first chapter introduces Nakos as I know her and sketches her life, including the circumstances of the writing of her major works and the themes that pervade them. The second chapter surveys her short stories. The following chapters discuss her major books in the order in which they were published, with a final chapter giving an overview of her work and its development over half a century.

Although I am a linguist, this book does not include a chapter on Nakos's language. Were I to write the book today, I would discuss in more depth the language question in Greece, and I would incorporate a close linguistic analysis of Nakos's style, to discover just how her writing is "conversational," as it has been called, by comparing it to her actual recorded conversation. I am about to undertake such a study. However, the first draft of the present book was written in 1975–76, before I became a linguist. It therefore reflects my earlier training and work in literary criticism.

Throughout the book, excerpts from Nakos's work and from the writings of Greek critics are my translations from the Greek editions cited. Quotations attributed to Nakos, unless otherwise cited, are my translations of my transcription of her comments to me in tape recorded conversation. Throughout the book, I

Preface

have avoided use of the generic masculine, except in cases where there was no other way to translate the Greek. Such cases, though few, are unfortunate since Nakos's writing never uses a generic masculine.

There are innumerable people to thank, without whom this book would never have materialized. I am grateful, first and always, to Mary Gianos, former editor of TWAS/Greece, who suggested I undertake this project and whose death before its completion caused me much personal grief as well as professional loss. I am always grateful, too, to George Paterakis, without whom I would never have learned Greek nor become involved in things Greek, and Mathilde Paterakis, my most devoted and beloved Greek teacher. Cleo and Manolis Helidonis and Rouli Ghemeni were my family in Greece while I worked on the first draft, and Cleo Helidonis has repeatedly performed emergency tasks in Athens, as has Carol Schoen in New York.

In addition, many generous and knowledgeable people read and commented on drafts of the manuscript: Tom Anselmo, Alton Becker, George Giannaris, Cleo Helidonis, John Hobbs, Maria Menke, June McKay, Thomas Noble, Livia Polanyi, Margaret Rader, and especially Thomas Doulis, who was also a source of crucial expert advice and invaluable encouragement. I wish to thank Rae Dalven for introducing me to Elli Alexiou, and Alexiou for introducing me to Nakos; Harry Weinreb for hours spent tracking down Nakos's early French stories in Paris libraries and for taking photographs; P. A. Mackridge and K. Steryiopoulos for directing me to sources; Jason Stavrakis for arranging use of an IBM typewriter in Athens; Rouli Ghemeni, Maria Menke, and Vaggelis Fragiadakis for emergency translation-assistance; and my teachers in literary criticism: Zack Bowen, John Hagopian, Robert Kroetsch, and Joseph Prescott. I want to thank Jim Edmund, a Clarence Darrow of a CPA; my parents, Dorothy and Eli Tannen; and, with all my heart, Lilika Nakos.

Deborah Tannen

Georgetown University

Chronology

1899	Ioulia Nakos born June 23 in Athens.[1]
1911	Moves to Geneva with mother.
1924–1929	Residence in Davos.
1928	"Photini" published in Paris. Greek translation, "*Foteini,*" published in Athens.
1929	Residence in Paris.
1930	Returns to Greece.
1932	*I Xepartheni* [The Deflowered One] published in Athens.
1933	Death of father. Employment as high school teacher in Crete.
1934–1938	Employment as high school teacher in Athens. Establishes puppet theater in Zappeion, Athens.
1934–1941	Employment as journalist by *Akropolis*.
1935	*Oi Parastratimenoi* [The Lost] published in Athens. Attends international anti-fascist writers' conference in Paris.
1936	*I Zoi tou Edgar Poe* [The Life of Edgar Poe] published in Athens.
1936–1940	Writes more than 20 fictionalized biographies serialized in newspapers.
1937	Marriage to Constantine Foskolos.
1938	Attends second anti-fascist writers' conference in Paris.
1938–1939	Trip to Sweden and Holland for *Akropolis*.
1939	Trip to Switzerland. Divorce.

LILIKA NAKOS

1941	Volunteer nurse during German Occupation of Greece.
1944	*I Kolasi Ton Paidion* [The Children's Hell] published in Alexandria, Egypt.
1945–1946	Employment as journalist by *Ethnos*.
1946	*The Children's Inferno* (English translation of French translation of stories from *The Children's Hell*) published in the United States.
1946–1947	Employment as journalist by *Embros*.
1947	Death of mother. Moves to Switzerland (Lausanne).
1953	Begins spending summers in Ikaria, Greece. *Nafsika* published in Athens.
1955	*I Kyria Ntoremi* [Mrs. Doremi] published in Athens. *Gi Tis Voiotias* [Boetian Earth] published in Athens under the title *Anthropina Pepromena* [Human Fate].
1955–1956	Employment as journalist by *Ora*.
1958	Retirement from journalism with pension from Journalists' Union.
1959	*I Kolasi Ton Paidion* [The Children's Hell] published in Athens.
1960	*Yia Mia Kainouryia Zoi* [Toward a New Life] published in Athens.
1963	*Oi Oramatistes Tis Ikarias* [Ikarian Dreamers] published in Athens.
1965	*Prosopikotites pou Gnorisa* [Personalities I Have Known] published in Athens.
1967	Stricken with paralysis in Ikaria. Resumes permanent residence in Greece.
1976	*Pote Pia* [Nevermore] published in Athens (previously published as *The Life of Edgar Poe*). *Toward a New Life* reprinted in Athens.
1978	*Human Fate* reprinted in Athens. *Oi Paragnorismenoi* [The Misunderstood] published in Athens.

Chronology

1979 *The Lost* serialized on Greek television. *Mrs. Doremi* reprinted in Athens.

1980 *To Chroniko Mias Dimosiografou* [Chronicle of a Journalist] published in Athens. *The Deflowered One* and *Nafsika* reprinted in Athens. *Personalities I Have Known* reprinted in Athens.

1981 *I Istoria tis Parthenias tis Despoinidas Tade* [The Story of the Virginity of Miss Tade], collected short stories, published in Athens. *Nevermore* reprinted in Athens.

1982 *Ikarian Dreamers* reprinted in Athens.

Chapter One
Restlessness and Commitment: Life and Times
Introducing Lilika Nakos

When I first called Lilika Nakos[1] because I was considering writing a book about her work, she arranged to meet me at the bus stop near her home in Halandri outside Athens. To help me recognize her she said, "I'm very little and a little fat" *(kontoula* and *pachoula).* Later, as I waited at the appointed bus stop, I saw a black-clad woman with a cane slowly navigating around the puddles in the unpaved road. When we stood before each other, she was half my height, looking up with a smile exposing five or six teeth huddled at the front of her mouth. We walked back to her house a few blocks away. Walking at her pace, we had time to talk. She told me that she preferred Halandri to Athens, but she was sad because her cats had left her after the move. She was pleased that I understood because, she said, Greeks generally didn't.

As we approached the house in which Nakos occupies the downstairs flat, she pointed out the word *AGAPI* ("LOVE") painted high on the concrete wall. That was one of the reasons she rented that house, she said. A brass plate on the gate announced: LILIKA NAKOS, JOURNALIST.

A recent encyclopaedia of modern Greek prose describes Nakos's home since 1931 as "a constant center of hospitality for suffering intellectuals and writer friends. Helping others is one of her weaknesses, perhaps to fill her lonely and nevertheless bohemian life."[2] The critic's lay analysis aside, this description characterizes Nakos aptly. Two small pensions—one from the journalists' union and one from the government because her father was a member of Parliament—support Nakos as well as a flock of young girls from Ikaria (relatives of one Ikarian girl whom Nakos employs as a helper), frequent friends and guests, and innumerable cats and dogs that have found their way to her hearth.

When Lilika Nakos sits on the frayed couch in her living room, her feet barely clear the edge. Always tiny, she is now shapeless with the extra weight of age. Her hair, dyed brown, is short in no particular style; the skin of her face is dark and leathery and incredibly wrinkled. She talks while the Ikarian girls move about the room clearing the dining table. When Nakos looks aside, by some strange effect, the blue of her eyes shimmers. She laughs. Her wit cuts through pretensions.

"I was the first hippie in Greece," Nakos remarks with a laugh. I heard tales of Nakos's eccentricity from her friends. One winter evening, for example, she couldn't find her scarf, so she knotted a woolen sock around her neck. Returning home that night, she carefully peeled it off and draped it on the hook with her coat. Another time, she didn't care if she went to an important lecture with a torn sleeve: "I'll sit in the back, and I won't take off my coat," she told her friend. But at the lecture she was quickly recognized and ushered to the first row. Then she felt warm, so she took off her coat, saying, "Oh, well . . ."

Nakos never tires of teasing her good friend Mrs. T., a retired archeologist. "Mrs. T. is a scientist," Nakos likes to say. "She has to have everything just so. It drives me crazy. I have to have things in a mess." The phone rings, and it is Mrs. T. herself. In the course of the conversation she tells Nakos that she is going to take a bath because she has an appointment with the doctor. "Why do you have to take a bath?" Nakos asks her, with a twinkle in her eye which Mrs. T. cannot see. "You're not going to sleep with him." After she hangs up, she repeats her joke several times under the guise of self-reproach. "Why did I say that? I'm terrible. Poor Mrs. T. I really upset her. I don't know why I said that: 'You're not going to sleep with him!' " She clearly enjoys her own irreverence.

This is Lilika Nakos, a novelist of the group of writers called "The Generation of the Thirties."[3] The critic Pericles Rodakis asserts that every woman writing in Greece today has been influenced by Nakos's style.[4] It would be more accurate to say that every person writing in Greece today has been influenced by her style. Nakos was one of the first women to write prose in Greek. In addition, her work was pioneering in two striking ways. First, she wrote with shocking frankness and beguiling simplicity about the most intimate experiences and emotions of her characters, furnishing, for the first time in modern Greek literature, a series of *bildungsromans* of women coming of age and coming to terms with sexuality. Second, Nakos accomplished this narrative task in a flow of conversational-sounding yet lyrical demotic language which suited perfectly the first-person point of view she preferred.

Thus Nakos contributed to the development of both the content and the form of the "social novel" in modern Greek, helping to throw off the yoke of *katharevousa,* the synthetic puristic language which had been the vehicle for Greek prose until the beginning of the twentieth century. One critic hailed Nakos's first Greek novella, *I Xepartheni* [The Deflowered One, 1932], as "one of the most important and creative efforts for the shaping of the modern Greek novel in its social aspect" because of the "boldness and frankness" with which it portrays the "many bitter truths of the upper-middle class" alongside the "psychological analysis of the characters, especially the women."[5]

A Sketch of Her Life

Ioulia Nakos (nicknamed Lilika) was born in Athens at the turn of the century to upper-class parents. Her father, Loukas Nakos, of a prominent family from the province of Leivadia, was a lawyer, published author, and socialist member of Parliament. Her mother, Eleni Papadopoulos, was from a wealthy, highly educated, and philanthropic Athenian family. As early as age six, Lilika lived for periods of time in Marseilles, France, and Genoa, Italy. When she was twelve, her mother took her to live permanently in Geneva, Switzerland, a city the child found drab and cold. Nakos describes the impact of this move on the child that she was:

This change, this uprooting, was a shock for the little girl. The ugly, rainy climate of Geneva, the loss of the beloved old house in Plaka with its spacious courtyards and cypress trees, the foreign language, the inhospitability of the residents, threw her into melancholy and made her long for Greece.[6]

Yet this move was not totally destructive. In Geneva, Lilika became closer to her mother, who had been preoccupied in Athens with the life of a society wife. Furthermore, growing up in Geneva afforded the great advantage of a Swiss education. Lilika graduated from high school, studied music at the Conservatory of Music in Geneva, and then took a degree in belles lettres from the University of Geneva. Finally, Nakos was exposed to a world view far broader than any she would have seen in Greece.

While still an adolescent, Lilika met the French writer Romain Rolland, author of the popular roman-fleuve *Jean Christophe,* and she worked with him for the International Red Cross during World War I. Geneva at this time was the center of much international pacifist and leftist political activity which influenced Nakos deeply. Furthermore, she was able to live a bohemian life which would have been unthinkable for an aristocratic young woman in Athens. She played piano at cafés, gave music lessons, and even for a time worked as a waitress in a Greek restaurant. Moreover, she had the chance to meet many European artists and intellectuals.

When she was only seventeen, Nakos met her father's friend George Ventiris, a leftist historian and close associate of the great Greek statesman Eleftherios Venizelos. She fell in love with Ventiris, and this love continued to motivate her personally as long as Ventiris lived. In a critical commentary published with *The Deflowered One,* Nakos's first novella published in Greece, Constantine Dimaras notes Ventiris' influence on her work and her thought. Ventiris was Nakos's only significant love, even though she married the sculptor Constantine Foskolos after Ventiris' death. This marriage was ended by divorce two years later.[7]

When Ventiris contracted tuberculosis and went to recuperate in the Swiss mountaintop town of Davos, Nakos accompanied him.[8] She lived there for most of the period between 1924 and 1929, nursing him and supporting herself by playing piano at movies and concerts. These, Nakos says, were the only years of her life when she was "relatively happy." It was then that she wrote her first stories, in French, and sent them to Paris where they were published in leading magazines. (During this time she also befriended Albert Einstein, who was in Davos teaching at a new university. This friendship is discussed in Nakos's memoir, *Prosopikotites pou Gnorisa* [Personalities I Have Known].)

In 1929 Ventiris left Davos for Paris. Nakos too descended from the Swiss town, and the couple lived together. Because they were not married, she was snubbed by the Parisian Greek society who entertained Ventiris. But she was warmly accepted by the French leftist literary group which clustered around Henri Barbusse, writer and publisher of the literary newspaper *Monde*[9] in which Nakos's first stories appeared. She found employment with Rieder Press, which published one novella of hers and gave her an advance on another. Her friends included such prominent writers as Andre Gide, Simone Weil, and Miguel de Unamuno.[10]

Nakos's return to Greece with Ventiris in 1930 cut short her French literary career. Nakos was not a stranger to Greece; she had been spending summers there, and was a member of the left-leaning literary group that gathered at the café at Dexameni near Kolonaki Square. The group included the writer Nikos Kazantzakis, his wife Galateia, and later her second husband Markos Avyeris, as well as her sister Elli Alexiou, the poets Kostas Varnalis and Sofia Papadakis, and, before his death in 1923, the important novelist Constantine Theotokis.

But being a summer visitor in Athens was different from living there permanently. The most immediate and significant change for Nakos was that she had to start writing in Greek rather than French. (Her first story to appear in Greece, "Photini," had been translated from the French by Galateia Kazantzakis). Nakos began by rewriting in Greek her stories and the novella *Le Livre de Mon Pierrot* [Petros's Book] which had placed first in an international contest sponsored by the newspaper *Le Petit Parisien* in 1928. Some of the stories were published together with the novella in 1932 under the title *I Xepartheni* [The Deflowered One], with an introduction by Ventiris.

By this time, however, Ventiris had lost interest in his young friend and had taken another lover. Nakos continued to be devoted to him just the same. The short stories she wrote at this time portray their young heroine as the wretched victim of uncontrollable love for a man grown indifferent to her. ("Love" and "Spring Invitation" were published in *Nea Estia* in 1933 and 1934, respectively).

Nakos's father died in 1933, leaving her and her mother no legacy except a pile of debts, and no means of support. Although Nakos had been writing for the newspaper *Ethnos,* she was paid negligible amounts for her work, and that only sporadically. So she unearthed her Swiss degrees in music and belles lettres and, taking advantage of her father's connections, got a job teaching music and French to nearly a thousand boys at the high school in Rethymnon, Crete. The most positive outcome of this experience was that it furnished the material for her novel, *I Kyria Ntoremi* [Mrs. Doremi], written fifteen years later. After a single harrowing year as one of two female teachers for the hordes of wild, even armed adolescent boys from the mountain villages of Crete, Nakos obtained a transfer to the Eighth Boys' High School of Athens.

At the Athens high school, Nakos was the only female faculty member. (A grown man who had been a student of hers then remembered only that when she sat on the podium teaching music, the boys concentrated on looking up her skirt.) Although her openly misogynous colleagues made teaching unpleasant, a secure job which included a hot meal at lunch was a great boon. Nakos's career as a teacher was brief, however. The story of her dismissal from the high school merits retelling, for it furnished material for her novel *Yia Mia Kainouryia Zoí* [Toward a New Life]. Moreover, it offers a glimpse of her temperament.

This was the era of the Metaxas dictatorship (1936–1941). Nakos was writing for the rightist newspaper *Akropolis*, even though her own political sympathies were critical of the fascist regime, because it was the only one whose editor would hire a woman. She had been sent to Sweden on assignment (the newspaper, incidentally, neglected to send her expense money, but that is another story, told in her memoir, *To Chroniko Mias Dimosiografou* [Chronicle of a Journalist].). Before leaving, Nakos had learned that the high school principal, in overzealous sympathy with the fascist regime, had denounced her along with all her liberal colleagues and many of the working-class students, to the security police.

Nakos took the opportunity to send the principal a postcard in which she informed him cheerfully, "I send you many regards from this free country of Sweden. The only black shadow here is your memory, which depresses me every time I think of it." She was not surprised when, shortly after her return to Greece, a messenger arrived at her house to deliver her dismissal notice. Both the messenger and her mother were incredulous when she welcomed him with open arms and a kiss: "Just what I've been waiting for!" ("I was a crazy girl," she commented as she told me the story.) How would she and her mother manage to eat thereafter? As for her interrogation by the police, who had the offending postcard in addition to the initial denunciation, when the chief of police regaled her with threats and insults in his office, he ended by saying that he would cut off her feet! She responded, "But I'm so short as it is. What will be left of me?" At this point he laughed and waved her away.

Although her flippancy indicates that Nakos was not easily intimated for her own welfare, it is clear that she did not take lightly the suffering and oppression of others. She presents a bitter portrait of the Metaxas era in *Toward a New Life*. As a result, she had a very hard time getting the novel published, and when it finally appeared in 1960, she was harassed by the police.

While she taught high school and after, Nakos continued to write for *Akropolis* and was fast becoming widely known for her *ftocholoyia:* muckraking articles about the downtrodden and unfortunate, especially workers, peasants, children, and women. Her first major journalistic assignment, to her mother's horror, was to interview prostitutes in Piraeus. Journalism was a far cry from the genteel life her mother had envisioned for her, but, with no other means of support, the mother could hardly object. Nakos herself, moreover, liked the work. Although she suffered ostracism by most of her colleagues since she was the only woman in Greek journalism then, yet she liked the hectic and earthy atmosphere of the newspaper office, and it gave her a chance to write. She began writing fictionalized biographies of famous people which were serialized in the newspaper.

Nakos, like most, lost her job during the German Occupation of Greece in 1941. She became a volunteer nurse at a makeshift hospital where children found dying of starvation in the street were brought to starve in the hospital instead. These children became the subjects of a series of short stories which Nakos wrote and smuggled, one by one, out of Greece. They were immediately published in Switzerland, where they awakened world consciousness to the great famine in Greece and were responsible for the first shipments of milk by the International Red Cross. Because of this concrete benefit, Nakos considers these stories her most important work. Collected under the title *I Kolasi Ton Paidion* [The Children's Hell], they were published in Alexandria (in Greek) in 1944. In 1946 a dozen of these stories were published in Lausanne in French translation as *L'Enfer des Gosses,* and all but one were published in English translation from the French as *The Children's Inferno* in the United States. Long since out of print, this is Nakos's only book available in English. The Greek stories, published separately in Greek journals after the war and as a book in Athens in 1959, were reprinted in 1971.

During the German Occupation Nakos and her mother starved and shivered like everyone else in Athens. So that they might eat, Nakos sold all their furniture and household goods on the black market, then took to the streets selling cigarettes. To this day she avoids the sun because of a head injury suffered when she was beaten by a German officer. Their home was routinely raided; any copies she had of her early publications were either lost or burned for warmth. One time, when the Germans were ready to kill her because she looked Jewish, Nakos was spared only because she was able to produce documents showing that her great-grandfather Nakos had been a provincial landowner who figured in the Revolution of 1821. "In the end," Nakos wrote of herself in the third person, "they were saved by the Red Cross, who found them, her mother and herself, collapsed from hunger on the floor of their house on Omirou Street."[11]

In the midst of this hell, Nakos discovered that she could temporarily dull the pain of hunger by pressing her knee into her stomach. In this position she wrote a second long novel, *Anthropina Pepromena* [Human Fate], later reprinted as *Gi Tis Voiotias* [Boetian Earth]. Through this book, she returned to the fairy-tale world of the province of Leivadia where she had spent happy childhood summers with her paternal grandfather.

Nakos's mother died in 1947 as a result of her starvation during the war. So did Nakos's ex-husband, Foskolos, and her half-brother and half-sister, her mother's children by a prior marriage whom she had met in adulthood and come to love. "I nearly died too," Nakos says in her offhand, good-humored manner, "but I didn't. Strange. Maybe I should have."

After the war there was no longer anything to keep Nakos in Athens. She took the small amount of money she had received from the Alexandrian edition of *The Children's Hell* and bought a ticket to Switzerland.

"It was the Civil War," Nakos told me, referring to the bitter battle that erupted in Greece following World War II, between Greek Communists and their opponents. "I left here *kakin-kakos* ["in a terrible state"]. I went to Lausanne and I didn't have anything to eat. I sat in a café, and a fellow I knew came by. 'Hey,' he said, 'the editor of *Illustré* wants you. He wants a story about Crete—a humorous one.' What, humorous?! I wasn't happy at all. But I didn't have anything—nowhere to sleep, nothing to eat, no room, nothing. He gave me an advance of 200 francs, I took a room, I ate, and I started to write." The result was her only comic novel, *En Crete,* based on her experiences teaching at the boys' high school in Rethymnon, which Nakos later rewrote in Greek as *I Kyria Ntoremi* [Mrs. Doremi].

Nakos lived in Switzerland and Paris from 1947 until 1955, writing for French language newspapers. Toward the end of this time she was stricken with back trouble that paralyzed her for days. A Swiss doctor advised her that the Greek climate would be more salutory, and that she should visit, particularly, the thermal springs on the island of Ikaria. Nakos didn't know where this island was; the doctor had to show it to her on a map. Taking his advice, she returned to Greece after her second long absence.

"I had forgotten Greece and her troubles," Nakos said. She took to spending summers on Ikaria, for she liked the poverty-stricken island. She found work writing for Athens newspapers during the winter until she retired from journalism in 1958. Eventually, Nakos began making plans to settle on the island of Ikaria. Her last major novel, *Oi Oramatistes Tis Ikarias* [Ikarian Dreamers, Athens, 1963], is about Greek-Americans returned to the island of Ikaria. However, Nakos's romance with the poor island was shattered and her interminable traveling between Europe and Greece came to a halt forever when she was struck by a paralyzing attack of sciatica at the Ikarian baths in 1967. After having spent twelve summers on the island, Nakos returned to Athens on a stretcher. Her condition improved to the point where she can walk with difficulty, aided by a cane. But she will never go near Ikaria again because of her fear that her attack was caused by overexposure to the thermal springs.

Lilika Nakos is grounded. Her eternal conflict is at last settled. She will spend the rest of her life in Greece. For Nakos has always been both drawn to and alienated from Greece. She was terribly lonely there as a young child; she grew up and lived more than thirty years in Western Europe. Moreover, Nakos experienced the contrast between the Greeks' rejection of her as a writer, teacher, and journalist because she was a woman, compared with her acceptance in France and Switzerland. And yet she is deeply bound to Greece. She missed her motherland painfully when she went to live in Geneva as a child; she loved one Greek man and married another; she made great sacrifices throughout her life in order to live and work in Greece.

Every summer Nakos has hopes of going to Corfu, but her health, or that of her friends, or her financial situation, always prevents the trip. Some summers she rents a small house on the island of Aegina near Athens to satisfy her longing for the sea.

When she first went to Ikaria, Nakos took in a village girl, Aspasia, who returned with her to Athens and lived with her for twelve years, until Aspasia's marriage in 1974. Now Nakos's home is filled with Aspasia's sisters and cousins who stay with Nakos, some temporarily, some more or less permanently. Nakos does not send people away. With these young guests and her many adopted cats, as well as old friends who visit and new friends from the neighborhood, Lilika Nakos makes her life in the Athens suburb of Halandri, occasionally visiting her family's decaying home in the more distant suburb of Ekali. She continues to write, having recently finished a second memoir *Chronicle of a Journalist,* a number of biographies of deceased friends, *Oi Paragnorismenoi* [The Neglected] and a new series of stories, as yet unpublished. Mostly she spends her mornings walking slowly through the unpaved streets of Halandri and evenings visiting her friend Mrs. T. Together they sit before the television. Mrs. T. invariably falls asleep, and Nakos, who says that she finds the shows silly, watches and laughs. At night, or if the weather prevents her going out, she reads. In summer she suffers badly from the heat. Winters she spends most of her time sitting in the hall next to a gas heater which she bought with the $100 she was paid for her memoir, *Personalities I Have Known.* Most of her friends have died. She does not permit anyone to take her picture.

A Woman Writing in Greece

Nakos is one of several women of The Generation of the Thirties who were among the first women to play important roles in Greek literature. All the women of Nakos's generation who wrote had special backgrounds. For example, Elli Alexiou and Galateia Kazantzakis, sisters from Crete, came from a rare literary family which yielded three generations of writers. Tatiana Stavrou was from Constantinople, where Greek culture had advanced far beyond that enjoyed in Greece proper. When women did write, they turned more often to poetry; the names of the poets Myrtiotissa, Melissanthi, Zoe Karelli, and Maria Polydouri are better known in Greece than those of any prose writers (with the exception always of Kazantzakis). Nakos herself was atypical, having been raised and educated in Geneva.

As Yianis Kordatos notes, before 1900 there were no Greek women writers because women were not educated in Greece. Kordatos explains, "The names of two women who occupy a place in modern Greek literature appear only at the end of the last century."[12] One of these is Nakos's own aunt, her mother's sister, Arsenoe Papadopoulos.

Yet having a literary aunt did not help Nakos in her career. She hardly knew Papadopoulos because of a virulent antipathy between the aunt and Nakos's father, because of political differences which focused on the language question. The aunt was an unbending Purist, and her father, a dedicated Demoticist. When I asked about her aunt, Nakos recalled a single meeting when she was very young, during which her aunt called her "the frog's daughter." "I don't know why," Nakos remarked in her mock-ingenuous way. "For some reason I didn't like that." Moreover, the antagonism he felt for his sister-in-law set Loukas Nakos even more firmly against the idea of his daughter becoming a writer.

Though she was not influenced by her aunt, Nakos attributes her literary bent to her mother who, like her sister Arsenoe, had been educated at the prestigious Hill School and then the Arsakeion, an institution of higher education for women which their father had helped to found. Mrs. Nakos, always buried in stacks of books like the mother in Nakos's novella *Nafsika,* engendered and encouraged a passion for reading in her daughter, giving books to Lilika against her husband's orders.

Despite his progressive politics and the fact that he wrote numerous political books, Loukas Nakos was opposed to his daughter's education and career because she was a woman. He was furious when her first story appeared in *I Proia* in 1928. Translated into Greek from the French by Galateia Kazantzakis,

"Photini" depicts a haunted, lonely child who despises her upper-class parents and is driven mad with revulsion when she hears the groans and sighs of their lovemaking in the bed next to hers. Loukas Nakos was even more shocked than the Greek reading public. He hurried to Paris and repaid the advance Rieder Press had given his daughter on her next book, threatening them with a lawsuit if they went ahead with publication. He told his daughter he would cut off her hands if she continued to write.

Lilika never considered obeying her father's injunction to stop writing, but his anger cost her bitterly. Nakos rarely dwells on her personal suffering. She refers to it, if at all, in passing and then in a light tone which belies the depth of her feelings. When I managed to locate the story "Photini" after much effort, I was annoyed to discover that Nakos seemed to know all about it (her reaction to most of the old stories I unearthed was surprise). When asked why she had not mentioned "Photini," she replied that she wanted to forget that story because it had turned her father against her. We are all heirs to his wrath, for the stories that Loukas Nakos prevented from being published never found their way into print and are lost.[13]

The opposition Nakos encountered from her father was only one manifestation of the difficulty she faced as a woman in Greek society. "If you're a woman in Greece," she remarked, as if she were saying something that amused rather than oppressed her, "you have to struggle a lot." As a high school teacher and as a journalist, Nakos was surrounded by openly hostile male colleagues. At the newspaper, the men taunted as they passed her in the hall, "To the kitchen! To the kitchen!" She reports that she replied in frustration, "But the kitchen has to be stocked with food."

Despite this oppressive atmosphere, Nakos found a podium in the press. The *Megali Enkyklopaideia Neoellinikis Logotechnias* [Great Encyclopaedia of Modern Greek Literature] reports that her "important contribution to journalism was her investigation of social issues, which made her known and loved throughout Greece."[14]

The Journalist as Engaged Writer

Nakos's writing is always concerned with social issues and individual suffering. Journalism and fiction, for Nakos, are not separate entities but different modes united by similar themes, techniques, and aims. Her themes are oppression and social injustice, loneliness and despair. The technique is a straightforward first-person narrative in a demotic language which is available to even uneducated readers; the narratives contain vivid sketches of real people expressing their deepest feelings. In Nakos's newspaper articles as in her fiction, periods of personal despair are reflected in social conditions and in descriptions of nature but are finally succeeded by a resurgence of hope.

Nakos is deeply committed to the notion of writing as a source of hope. George Ventiris comments in his introduction to *The Deflowered One*, "The theory of Art for Art's Sake seems monstrous to her." Nakos says that she has written a piece called "The Murderers of the Soul," in which she criticizes writers who preach despair, including Kazantzakis. "And Sartre did bad, throwing people into despair. Into despair is easy. The feat is to bring them out of despair. Christ was great. He extracted a solution. He showed a road. It's agony if you don't believe in anything. Is it necessary to shout it?"[15]

Nakos herself as a child was torn between her father's skepticism and the superstitious belief of the village-bred servants who raised her. As a young woman, Nakos tended toward disbelief, but as she grew older she became more interested in religious and then mystical forces. While living in Davos, the lofty Swiss sanatarium town, she had the first of a number of mystical experiences in which she sensed a connection with larger forces and a deep sense of purpose. While her later novels show much preoccupation with mystical elements, the influence of religious concerns can be seen even in her early work. Today Nakos's favorite book, which she reads nightly, is *The Autobiography of a Yogi* by Yogananda. During the first years of our friendship Nakos seemed more interested in steering me toward this Yogi's work than toward her own.

In keeping with her concern for spiritual commitment and her belief that art should uplift, Nakos particularly values her series of fictionalized biographies, mostly written between 1936 and 1940, which were featured in installments in *Akropolis* and other Athenian newspapers and magazines. While depicting the lives of such famous people as Pasteur, Peter the Great, and Zola, Nakos incorporated her favorite themes and techniques. It gives her great satisfaction that these biographies—at least twenty of them, written in the early morning hours before Nakos went off to teach at the high school—reached a popular audience that did not read books. She tried, she says, to show the "good" side of her subjects in these serials, in order to edify her readers who had no other means of education. She attempted also to educate them in such areas as health and hygiene, for example, by writing at length about Pasteur's germ theory and about Paul Ehrlich's research into the causes of syphilis.

Major Themes in the Novels

Nakos's concern with giving hope is evident in her journalism. It is evident in her fiction as well, but at times the encouraging message is unconvincing, as if superimposed on the pessimism endemic to the novels, especially the early works which are almost Naturalistic in their tone and structure. It is as if hope is at odds with the faithful portrayal of the social and personal conditions Nakos experienced. As "social novels," Nakos's works interweave recurrent personal themes with the dramatization of a social milieu which reflects and exacerbates the characters' internal conflicts.

One of the most striking of these personal themes is related closely to the social aspect of the novels. The heroines of a number of Nakos novels are, like the author, caught between two classes that are at odds in society. Katina, the protagonist of *The Deflowered One*, is a member of the upper class, but her father refuses to give her any money, so she must work to support herself and her hidden illegitimate son. As a guest at her half-sister's fancy dinner party, Katina must listen to a stuffy, self-satisfied upper-class man rail against women who work (and especially women who write). A similar conflict is experienced by Alexandra, the heroine of Nakos's next major work and first full-length novel, *Oi Parastratimenoi* [The Lost].

Another theme recurrent in Nakos's work is expatriation, a condition which has always been of central significance to Greeks, who have perennially sent their children to live abroad. As has been seen, Nakos herself was an expatriate until she was thirty, and again at various periods throughout her life. The experience of living in Western Europe as a foreigner has had a lasting effect on her. The lyrical novella *Nafsika* describes with disturbing clarity the experiences of a child taken by her mother to live in Marseilles (as was Nakos at the age of six); *The Lost* depicts the lives of a group of foreigners living in a *pension* in Geneva (as did Nakos as a girl); *Ikarian Dreamers* comes full circle by portraying the homecoming of expatriate Greek-Americans.

Related to the expatriate experience, a significant and recurring theme in Nakos's work is the isolation of the individual and the drive to obliterate isolation through love. Nakos's early stories written in French, the later stories in *The Children's Hell;* and the first part of *The Lost* all concern desperately lonely children utterly isolated in a grown-up world. Although they are older, the heroines of *The Deflowered One* and *The Lost* are also hopelessly isolated, although Alexandra, in the latter work, finds purpose and love in the end by adopting her dead brother's child. In the later works connection through love becomes more possible: Barbara in *Boetian Earth* has deep rapport with both her grandfather and her companion Thanasis. In the sequel to this work, *Toward a New Life,* Barbara falls happily in love with Thanasis. The last work, *Ikarian Dreamers,* is optimistically romantic about the happily-ever-after marriage which ends the novel.

Ikarian Dreamers brings to resolution a number of themes that constitute the crucial conflicts throughout Nakos's work. Whereas in the earlier works love is "a scourge" tormenting its victims, here the issue of love is resolved, and marriage becomes possible. The expatriation theme is also happily resolved, through the homecoming of Ikarian-born Americans. Two other major themes are fused and worked out in this last novel: escapism and the conflict over ambivalence toward Greece.

For the remainder of this chapter each of these major themes will be discussed in light of Nakos's life. The chapters that follow will trace the development of these themes in each of the novels.

The Theme of Class Conflict

Throughout her life, Lilika Nakos has been pinned between the aristocratic upper class she was born into and the struggling working class into which she was thrust by economic necessity. Her ambivalence is evident. In her conversation as in her writing she extols the peasant class. Yet she remarks, with disdain, that today's Athenians are really villagers (and that, in contrast, her mother's family were true Athenians); she "corrects" the speech of the Ikarian girls in her house when they use village expressions. When confronted with my observation that the way they talk is "correct" for their dialect, she changed her admonition: "Now you're in Athens. Talk like Athenians!"

Confusion over class identity has its roots in Nakos's upbringing. Her parents were aristocratic. When she spent summers visiting Greece, Nakos liked to ride down Stadiou Street, the main artery of Athens, in her family's one-horse carriage. Elli Alexiou, Nakos's friend and fellow writer, told me of visiting Nakos as a young woman in her parents' fine Athenian house where tea was served in china cups, and Lilika played the piano for guests.

Despite this decidedly aristocratic upbringing, Nakos's father was an ardent socialist. He was the founder and president of the *Etaireia Dikaiomaton tou Anthropou* ("Association for Human Rights"). He was involved in the *Ekpaideftikos Omilos* ("Educational Association"), the important demoticist lobby, and was one of the closest associates of Alexander Papanastassiou, the founder of Greek socialism. When Lilika was a little girl, Eleftherios Venizelos, the hero of leftist democrats, was her father's dinner guest at their home in Plaka. As an adult in Davos, Nakos spent many hours with Venizelos who regularly visited their mutual friend, Ventiris. Thus from her father, and later from his friend and her lover George Ventiris, Nakos absorbed a distinctly leftist political orientation, even though she never actively engaged in political activities.

In a deeper sense, Nakos became a member of the working class. First her father cut off her support because he disapproved of her life style; then he died, leaving his wife and daughter nothing but debts. As has been seen, Nakos supported herself and her mother as a journalist. In addition, she worked as a high school teacher, a pianist, a puppeteer, a nurse, a salesclerk in a bookstore, and a waitress. She gained firsthand experience of the hardships of working people.

The Geneva where Nakos came of age and lived as a young woman was a center for expatriate Russian revolutionary activity. The influence of this milieu upon her is described in her memoir *Personalities I Have Known*. The atmosphere of revolutionary idealism in pre-World War I Geneva is re-created in *The Lost* as well. Even after she returned to Greece, Nakos maintained her ties with many of the influential French writers of the Left, and in 1935 and 1938 she attended international anti-fascist writers' conferences in Paris.

Although not actively aligned with any political group, Nakos has always had a keen awareness of class struggles and a concern for the oppressed. All her works depict with accurate poignancy the suffering of the working poor and the complacency of the upper classes. When she creates Communist characters, they are idealistic and sympathetic people who have compassion for others. But while approving of them as people, Nakos stops short of endorsing their political philosophy, which her heroines invariably profess not to understand, and against which other sympathetic and sensible characters argue convincingly. Today Nakos has little patience with Communist ideology and dogma.

The Theme of Greek Identity

From the age of six when her mother took her to live for a time in Genoa, Italy, until 1967 when she was struck by a crippling illness at the thermal springs on the island of Ikaria, Lilika Nakos traveled back and forth between Western Europe and Greece. "Everyone has their weakness," she once remarked. "That was mine. Coming and going." The ease with which she traveled back and forth reflected and aggravated the conflict Nakos experienced between the pull of Greek tradition and the lure of Europe.

A preoccupation with the meaning of "Greekness" figures prominently in the work of the entire Generation of the Thirties.[16] Disillusionment with Greece during this period was exacerbated by the 1922 Asia Minor disaster, called by Greeks simply The Catastrophe: no other could compare to it. Until 1922 Greeks considered the process of liberation of Greek land from Turkish rule to be still under way. They were inspired by the *Megali Idea,* the "Great Idea" that Greece would reoccupy the territory that had constituted the Byzantine Empire, with a Greek capital at Constantinople. In 1922 the Turks, having secretly rearmed following their defeat in World War I and having grown strong under the dynamic leadership of Mustafa Kemal (Ataturk), repelled the Greek army which had entered Turkey as belated agents of Allied occupation. The Turks took this opportunity to rid their land of residents of Greek and Armenian descent. The expulsion, carried out in a particularly brutal way, dumped on Greek shores hordes of refugees, many of whom had never before set foot in Greece, for they came from Greek communities that had developed independently of mainland Greece in the cosmopolitan cities of Asia Minor. The re-rooting of nearly a million and a half people (almost a quarter of Greece's population at the time) forced all Greeks to reevaluate their culture, their traditions, and their significance as a small country lying beside modern Europe and the Balkans.[17] They were dazed, casting about for self-respect in a new image, coming to terms with the demise of their Great Idea of a Greece reconstituted in the image of Byzantine glory.

This conflict about Greek identity is at the core of all Nakos's work. Each of her novels is, in a sense, an exploration of the issue of Greece's identity and its place in modern Europe. The attitude toward Greece that emerges is rather like that of an angered lover: Nakos rails against the suffering that modern Greece causes her people (reminiscent of James Joyce's characterization of Ireland as a sow who eats her farrow) at the same time that she romanticizes Greece's ancient heritage and peasant spirit.

Thomas Doulis observes, "The Generation of the Thirties and even older writers like Nikos Kazantzakis and Kostas Varnalis, found themselves less interested in the native traditions and more apt to find their inspiration in foreign (i.e., European) sources. This continued throughout the decade of the 1930's."[18] Similarly, Nakos's work during this early period tends to be concerned with her life in Europe and is correspondingly critical of Greece, reflecting as well the negative self-image that she developed as a foreigner in Switzerland.

Nakos's examination of what it meant to be Greek was rudely initiated when she arrived in Geneva at the age of twelve. Her own first experience of Swiss prejudice is adapted as an episode in *The Lost,* when the heroine, Alexandra, arrives at a Swiss hotel with her mother.

I heard a gentleman whisper to the hotel owner: "What are they? New ones?"

"Yes" said the owner with a grimace full of scorn. "They're Balkans..."

. . .

"Oh, well. You can't throw customers out!"

That's all I managed to hear... I even tripped on the step. I thought to myself: Balkans! What does "Balkans" mean? It was the first time I'd heard that word. I didn't know we were Balkans! And why that scornful air?[19]

Nakos recalls furthermore that, as a child in Swiss schools, she was made to sit in a special section with other foreign children, apart from the Swiss, and that no Swiss children ever befriended her or invited her into their homes. During these early experiences of the Swiss scorn for her Greekness, she did not feel a compensating Greek pride. Her early works portray Greece as a stultifying and unenlightened place.

The turning point came for Nakos, as it did for her compatriots, during the German Occupation. Peter Bien explains this phenomenon in his discussion of the works of Nikos Kazantzakis, another Greek writer who lived many years in Europe.

. . . for the Greek people's suffering and resistance during this period gave them a unity and dignity that had been lacking in the years following the Asia Minor catastrophe. These events caused not only Kazantzakis but many other Greek writers to change their styles, and themes, to deepen their national consciousness, to recapture knowledge of the peasant culture and thus find their own roots. [20]

The two works that Nakos wrote during the German Occupation represent two opposite ways of responding to the grim conditions of the Occupation. *The Children's Hell* depicts the holocaust around her, while *Boetian Earth* constitutes an escape from it. Nevertheless, both works take pride in the Greek people and wax romantic about their heritage. This rather chauvinistic spirit is the one that prevails, and it dominates Nakos's last novel, *Ikarian Dreamers*.

Isolation and Loneliness

"A person lives all alone," writes Nakos in her most optimistic novel, *Ikarian Dreamers*, "a stranger to the person beside him, and great is his loneliness" (128). Virtually all the main characters in Nakos's works suffer from this realization.

The roots of Nakos's preoccupation with the theme of personal isolation may lie in the fact that she lived her own life very much alone. It has been seen how keenly she felt her apostasy as a foreign child in Geneva. Even before that, while a young child in Greece, she felt alienated from her parents. Her father was busy with his law practice, his politics, his girl friends. Her mother had her society life. Nakos's early stories re-create the sense of suffocation she felt in the asphyxiating upper-class household, reflected in the devastating heat of the Athens summer.

As a child, Lilika looked to the servant girls for company, but they resented the little rich girl. Nakos illustrated this resentment by recalling the following memory. A servant girl, having overheard Lilika's mother telling the child a honey-coated birds-and-bees story, called Lilika aside as soon as the mother departed. "Don't listen to that nonsense!" she snapped. Clapping her hand to her crotch, she rudely set the child straight: "That's where you came from! In goes the pole and out comes the baby!"

It is not surprising that in Nakos's fictional world parents are often geographically and always spiritually distant from their children who seek and sometimes find love and (temporary) connection with grandparents, nursemaids, or strangers.

The Lure of Greece

The tilt in favor of Greece and away from glorifying Europe in Nakos's fiction reflects the author's own decision to settle finally in her motherland. One can't help wondering why she forsook a promising career in Paris to return to Greece in 1930, and again left Switzerland where she had made a comfortable home after 1947. Why did she stop writing in French, the language of her education and the one in which she felt most comfortable, to write in Greek, a language she knew only from her home and her earliest years at school and which might be read, at best, by a few intellectuals among the few people in the world who knew Greek? Moreover, she left a country where she had already begun to earn a living with her pen, in order to go to one where even recognized writers had to work doubly hard at other occupations in order to pay for the publication of their work, a country where life was difficult for anyone who worked, even more so for a writer, and inexpressibly so for a woman writer. Although she returned to Europe many times, often with the intention of staying permanently, Greece continued to draw Nakos irresistibly back to its shores. Why?

Nakos herself says that she returned to Greece in 1930 because Ventiris, the man she loved, went back. Then, she says, she had the responsibility of supporting her mother who hated living abroad. (But all the years her mother chose to live in Geneva? I ask. Yes, says Nakos, but her mother never liked it. It had been the only way she could respectably separate from her husband, since she had already been divorced once.) The second time Nakos went back to Greece it was on the advice of a Swiss doctor. Then she visited the springs at Ikaria and became attached to this poor Aegean island.

These reasons must indeed have influenced her decisions. What may be the deepest reason for her repatriation, however, becomes focused in her friendship with the great Spanish writer Miguel de Unamuno, whom Nakos knew in Paris in 1929. Unamuno was exiled from the Ribera dictatorship in Spain. When she told him that "I never felt like a stranger in Paris nor among the French, that I expressed myself—at that time—more easily in French," Unamuno's response was "almost threatening," as Nakos reconstructs his words in her memoir:

"And don't you blush to say that, so lightly, as a Frenchman would say it! I can see, my girl, you don't understand what it means to be Greek, to derive from such a glorious race. . . . Yes, and your language—doesn't it mean anything to you that it's the language of the Gods, and you dare to say you express yourself more easily in French! You know that the language you speak today in Greece, your demotic, is the daughter and flesh of the ancient Greek language, and that it's one of the most beautiful and richest languages of Europe: and you sit and write in a borrowed language: overworked, fixed, pre-formed, ready to slip like a glove on anyone who studies it... You prefer the foreign glove on your hand rather than stretching out your arms and embracing the sea, the Greek sea." (56–57)[21]

Nakos portrays Unamuno as insistent and loquacious. Even more powerful, however, is the impact of his own example. She presents him speaking of "his Spain, just as a lover speaks of his beloved" (48). His bitter suffering is palpable, as is his inconsolable sense of isolation among the French and the desperate longing for his own land which finally drive him to leave Paris for the Spanish border, to gaze upon his homeland if only from afar. This longing for homeland is at the heart of Nakos's last novel, *Ikarian Dreamers*, re-created in the emotions of the Greek-Americans in Ikaria.

Perhaps most significant of all is Unamuno's observation about the nature of Nakos's writing:

"And you, a Greek, sit and write French? I've read your stories. The theme, the atmosphere is Greek... All your being—without your realizing it—has its roots in Greece." (57)

Unamuno impressed upon Nakos the fact that she needed to write in Greek because her work sought to capture, through dialogue and description, the spirit of the Greek people and the atmosphere of Greece. Peter Bien explains this same phenomenon as it was experienced by Kazantzakis, who tried in vain to write in French for financial reasons, but found his novels had to be written in Greek. Even though Nakos's French was, for all practical purposes, native, she needed demotic Greek as a vehicle for her writing just as much as Greek literature needed her. The conflicts and concerns she would work out in her art were bound up with Greece, and she was committed to the genre of the novel, which is woven from the daily lives and voices of the people portrayed. Perhaps this, then, is why Unamuno's exhortation took root and Nakos "obeyed him," as she puts it, returning to her homeland to take her place in Greek literature among the writers of the Generation of the Thirties who were grappling with the very issues that the circumstances of her life had forced her to confront.

Lilika Nakos has written nine novels, an assortment of stories, and more than twenty fictionalized biographies reflecting her times. Her times span the half-century from pre-World War I Geneva *(The Lost)* and Greece *(Boetian Earth),* covering the pre-World War II Metaxas dictatorship *(Toward a New Life)* and the German Occupation *(The Children's Hell),* to the modern era of atomic bombs and cold war *(Ikarian Dreamers).* Their settings range from the Athens of her first novella *(The Deflowered One),* through the Greek island where *Nafsika* begins, to Marseilles where it ends, and to the rocky mountains of Crete in *Mrs. Doremi.* All these novels are peopled by skillfully drawn characters engaged in a rapid succession of striking incidents. The impact of the novels hinges on the unfolding of events; the characters, who emerge if not in psychological complexity yet in emotional depth, are revealed through their responses to these events, which combine with the characters to constitute a vast social document as well as the author's contribution to the shaping of the modern Greek novel.

Chapter Two

Loneliness and Hunger: Short Stories

Lilika Nakos is primarily a novelist, but she has also written short stories, mostly early in her career.[1] Nakos's first publications were stories written and published in French in Paris and Switzerland, before 1930. Her first Greek publication was a story translated from the French by Galateia Kazantzakis in 1928. Nakos began her Greek literary career in 1930 by translating her early stories into Greek. (Five of these were translated into English from the French by Allan Ross Macdougall, who had them published in small American literary magazines between 1934 and 1941.) Some appeared in Greek literary magazines, and some were published along with a Greek rewriting of her first novella, *The Deflowered One*. During World War II Nakos wrote a series of stories depicting children starving to death during the German Occupation in Athens in the winter of 1941. These seventeen stories have been published as a collection entitled *I Kolasi Ton Paidion* [The Children's Hell] and have been translated into a number of languages, including English. After World War II Nakos wrote exclusively novels, until recently when she has again turned to writing short stories.

Nakos's stories are short, usually only a few pages, and, whether narrated in the first or third person, they generally reflect the single point of view of their protagonists. Most often the story creates a vivid atmosphere through a situation that leads quickly to a striking event, either climaxing or reversing the atmosphere created until that point.

The stories fall into three main categories. Most of them are about children who are lonely and alienated in an adult world.

Others portray miserable victims of love. The rest, which also often have child protagonists, depict personal suffering that is caused by social conditions. The stories of the latter category include those that have been collected and published under the title *The Children's Hell*.

The Social Story

The Asia Minor disaster discussed in Chapter One is one of the most significant influences on Greek fiction of the 1930s in Greece. Nakos treats this subject directly in her story "Maternity" which won her an award and early recognition in Switzerland and has been repeatedly anthologized in an English translation from the French.[2] "Mitrotis" [Maternity] concerns the dilemma of a 14-year-old Armenian boy in a refugee camp in Marseilles set up for Armenians and Greeks who have escaped from Turkey. The boy's mother has died in childbirth, and he has strapped to his back the newborn infant which has been howling with hunger for days. After much searching and suffering, the boy finds in the Greek refugee camp a nursing mother who seems disposed to help him. She asks to see the baby, and other Greek women gather around as well. But upon seeing the infant, they all shriek in horror. The baby has become grotesque from starvation. The women call the baby a devil and drive the boy out of their camp. As he sits weeping and hopeless, a Chinese street merchant, who has been taunted by the children in the camp, appears and leads away the reluctant boy, who expects only further harm, having heard that the Chinese, like the Jews, drink Christian blood. But he finds himself in a home: a veritable Shangri-la of peace and love which contrasts miraculously with the squalor of the refugee camp. The delicate and gentle Chinese wife shows him her own blissful infant. She too emits a cry when she sees the shriveled Armenian baby, but hers is a cry of sympathy, as she takes the starving mouth to her breast.

The structure of this story replicates one that Nakos favors in her novels as well. The boy's hopes are dashed, suddenly and dramatically, but in the depth of his despair a new hope glimmers, and the story ends with unexpected salvation. The maternity of the title refers to the true mothering instinct of the adolescent boy and the Chinese couple, in contrast to the lack of maternity of the Greek mother. Besides portraying the boy's dilemma, the story is a lesson in ethnic tolerance and a witness to the Asia Minor refugee experience.

Another story with a didactic impact is "O Tycheros" [The Lucky One]. (This story appeared in English under the title "The Son").[3] Iannis has returned from prison, and his wife is delighted and stunned by his homecoming. When she reluctantly leaves him to rest, he recalls the circumstances of their meeting and marriage. Iannis found her when he was about to sneak out of the country to escape the police. She too was being chased, by villagers, having been expelled from the brothel where she worked because she refused to have an abortion and could no longer bear to be touched by men. Iannis spontaneously offered to marry her, and immediately after the wedding he turned himself in to the police. As she visited him regularly in prison, he grew to love her child; now that he has returned, he is happy, although he realizes that he does not know his wife at all. The child is the saving force, for both husband and wife. (A child plays a similar role at the end of Nakos's first novel, *The Lost*.)

The social theme underlying "The Lucky One" is one Nakos often reiterated in her journalism as well as her fiction. The woman is a victim, a poor village girl sent to work as a servant in town. She was deflowered by the man of the house and then thrown out into the street when the fact became known to his wife. This specific scenario is one that recurs often in Nakos's writing.

Another story concerning a mistreated village girl is one of Nakos's best, "To Doulaki" [The Little Servant] portraying with clarity and passion the dramatic peaks and plunges of joy and despair experienced by a young child. In telling the story of Kyriakoula, a village girl taken as a servant by an Athenian family, Nakos introduces a number of themes that figure prominently in her later work: the contrast between the paradisiacal village and the hellish city; the isolation of the individual in an alien world; the mistreatment of the poor child by her heartless wealthy employees.

"The Little Servant" begins with Kyriakoula fantasizing that she is back on her beloved island of Ikaria, talking to her favorite sheep Moscho. She is abruptly wrenched back to the deadly atmosphere of Athens and the middle-class house in which she is exploited. Her mistress accuses the harassed and exhausted child of having stolen a silver spoon. The lady's threats drive Kyriakoula to mounting desperation; she believes the police will carry her off, a shame to her mother and her village. Phantasmagoric little spoons dance before her eyes. That evening, the lady sends her to get a bottle of wine cooling in the well whose black spirit has always terrified her.[4] At the well Kyriakoula hears steps approaching her from inside the house. At the same time, a gentle voice calls to her from the well, assuring her he is a benevolent spirit, full of light. Kyriakoula's persecution at the hands of her employers is fused with the universal human condition:

Oh, what loneliness this is for a poor little child. It's loneliness that kills young and old!... The soul's loneliness poisons, oh, how is Kyriakoula to escape the vast loneliness that encircles her. (66)[5]

As will be seen in Nakos's novels, the use of the present tense and repeated pauses; the repetition of the word *loneliness* interlaced with the repetition of her name heard houndingly from the house and soothingly from the well; the steps insistently nearing, closing in on her—all these combine to re-create the child's terror and render comprehensible her suicide by jumping into the well.

The Terrible World of Children

When children suffer, they suffer utterly. Many of Nakos's most effective stories are concerned with the suffering of children. "Photini," her first story published in Greece, re-creates with terrifying effectiveness the sense of asphyxiation and isolation experienced by a young girl in the home of upper-class parents whom she hates. In the end, the child is driven mad by spending the night pressing a pillow over her head in an attempt to block out the sounds of her parents making love in the bed beside hers.

A similar atmosphere pervades the story "O Thanatos tis Chrysas" [Chrysa's Death] also about a child who feels alienated from her parents, but Chrysa has one friend in the world: her baby sister. The story ends when Chrysa discovers that this sister has died. A similar loss is experienced by the protagonist of "O Nothos," [The Bastard] a little girl who is terribly lonely until she overhears that she has a half-brother, her father's illegitimate son. The little girl carefully plans a joyful reunion with her brother. At the end, however, when she manages to locate the boy and make her way to his house in the poor section of town, she sees through the window that he is very ill, and when she knocks on the door, the boy's mother recognizes her and sends her away, hurling curses after her.

Loss of love and alienation from an upper-class parent are also the themes of "The Broken Doll," a story available only in the English translation from the French. The child protagonist is alienated from her rich father, but she adores her mother (a situation that underlies the plot of the novella *Nafsika*), who has taken her to live in Marseilles in order to escape the father's cruelty. Just as the child has happily received a new doll from her mother, two Greek men appear and snatch her away to take her back to her father. The child is torn, struggling and crying, from her mother, who continues to run down the street after the disappearing car, holding the broken doll out before her.

The image of a child being cruelly led away figures in another story also. Told from the point of view of a little boy, "Kai to Paidi Eipe Psemata" [And the Child Lied] concerns the boy's sister, Marika, whose drama is poignantly and obliquely portrayed without her appearing in the story at all. In fact, her palpable absence contributes to the impact of her tragedy. The brother, Andreas, is not a child victim, but a perpetrator of injustice. He watches secretly as his sister is marched off to a convent between two nuns. The nuns are described, not the sister, who has already been dismissed by her family.

The sister has been beaten and sent to a convent because of her brother's fabrication that he saw the hotel cook "holding Marika naked on his lap" and "touching her all over... And she was laughing and kissing him on the mouth..." (28). The effect of his words was not foreseen by the boy. His motive was rather "to show his mother that he wasn't a baby any more... That he knew very well about these 'things' " (28). It is the mother who is really responsible, and the society that created and condoned her hysterical response, so that a child's thoughtless lie becomes the cause of his sister's total ostracism.

The boy's fantasies have succeeded no doubt beyond his most cherished oedipal fantasies; in the end, the boy is in his mother's warm embrace as she whispers to him, "Andreas, now it's just the two of us..." (29). The Freudian knot is tied at both ends: she too seems to relish being alone with her son. In this sense, this story prefigures the novel *The Lost*, in which a mother sends her daughter away because she cares only for her son.

Another story with a male protagonist, and another in which a child is shown as desperately alienated from his parents, is "Fotia Sto Spiti" [The House on Fire]. The protagonist of this story, also named Andreas, is so enraged at his parents that he runs away from home, feigning suicide—but first he elaborately fantasizes setting fire to the family home (an expression of rage that is put into action by the character Nikos in the novel *The Lost*).

Children and Sex

"And The Child Lied" is one of a number of early works in which Nakos explores the issue of girls and sexuality. However, this story does not focus directly on the little girl's trauma (as does the narrative of *The Deflowered One* in a scene of childhood molestation). The girl's suffering in this story emerges indirectly, as the maid reports that the little sister did not cry as they led her away, but simply looked dazed. The child's innocence sets in relief the perversity of the society that persecutes her—and the mother who represents that society.

A girl's introduction to sexuality is the main focus of "Akatanomastos" [The Nameless One]. As in many Nakos works, there is a gulf of indifference between the girl Marina and her mother. Marina says that she doesn't want her sick mother to die, "But at bottom I didn't care that much" (17). Her main preoccupation is her hatred for her mother's lover, less out of jealousy than out of a young girl's resentment of the male pose which she is still too young to be charmed by. When the boyfriend enters Marina's room and begins to fondle her leg, she feels faint but does not stop him at first. "I let his hand go higher. Suddenly I felt his hot breath, near my neck." Her delayed reaction is fierce and is marked by a shift to the present tense: "I turn, and trembling with repulsion, I spit in his face" (16).

This incident is only the first trauma. The maid Asimina shows Marina her mother's aborted fetus. Like an evil witch, in Greek folklore as in other Nakos books, Asimina sits under a fig tree laughing maliciously. The freakish unborn brother is the nameless one of the title, but so too is the mother's lascivious lover. He is called simply "the gentleman" by Asimina and "my mother's lover" by Marina. Both nameless ones haunt Marina that night. She trembles before the icons, feeling again the hot breath on her neck. In her sleep, she dreams of the Holy Virgin holding not the baby Jesus but the aborted fetus. In the morning Marina hides beside the road, and when the lover passes, she hurls a rock at him with all her strength. The last image of the story is his face covered with blood. Marina's attack represents a unique expression of feminine outrage. Other Nakos heroines are dazed and traumatized but do not strike back.

Another story that treats the issue of a young woman's introduction to sex is "I Istoria tis Parthenias tis Despoinidas Tade" [The Story of the Virginity of Miss Tade] which became the title story when Nakos's early stories were anthologized in 1981. Like the two previous stories, it was first written in French and later reprinted in Greek along with the first edition of *The Deflowered One*. "Miss Tade" has the meaning "Miss-So-and-so" or "Miss Doe." (In French it was "Demoiselle Une Telle.") The heroine is a young Greek woman who is visiting the man she loves in Switzerland, but is about to give up her virginity to another man. This was the first story Nakos wrote, and it apparently is set in Davos, where she wrote it.

The emptiness felt by a young woman in a strange land, about to relinquish her virginity to a man she hardly knows, is mirrored in the bare hotel room. Its third-person interior monologue reveals the young woman's thoughts as she sits on the edge of the bed awaiting the strange man's arrival. She is forcing herself to this unlikely initiation into sex with the doctor who informed her that she has hereditary syphilis, in order to satisfy herself that it is not contagious. The terrified girl longs for the man she really loves as she bids goodbye to "the dreams, the childhood dreams... white bridal veils, a church full of incense, the bed with lace decorated by her mother... erotic night in my country, in my own country..." (14).

The title of the story reflects the heroine's alienation from herself, as she is suspended between her romantic visions of sex and its impending opposite reality.

Mood Stories

The last of the three stories published in the first edition of *The Deflowered One* also takes place in Davos. Titled "To Koudouni" [The Bell], it focuses on a single small event: the ringing of the emergency bell in the middle of the night by a patient in a Swiss sanatorium. The story, like a number of others, does not recount a series of events but rather creates a mood.

The patient in "The Bell" is a young Greek woman, Liza, who is cheerful and warm, like many Nakos heroines. Although she is not inclined to dramatize her condition, Liza is jarred by the salt taste of blood in her mouth and its red stain on the sheets. The third-person narrative examines as well the minds of the other patients who are thus forced to confront the possibility of their own deaths. The story simply establishes the atmosphere of the sanatorium and the emotional states of its inhabitants in response to the bell.

Another story portraying a state of mind rather than a series of events is "Agapi" [Love], one of two stories which seem closely related to the novel *The Lost* in their depiction of a woman hopelessly in love with a man who has lost interest in her. The heroine of both "Love" and "Anoixiatiki Kalesma" [Spring Invitation] is named Elena, and the third-person narratives present her self-ironic perspective, as if she were watching herself with a snicker. Although she knows she has become a pest to the man she loves, Elena cannot shake off her passion to see him, even if just for a moment.

The poignancy of the story derives from Elena's own realization that she is ridiculous and her inability to act otherwise. When her ex-lover's friends come in, "Then Elena felt she had no right to be taking up space. She became a tiny little ball on her chair." Nakos shifts to the present tense and uses repeated pauses to communicate the intensity of Elena's discomfort: "She doesn't know what to say or what to do... But she can't unstick herself from the chair... She starts making jokes... But no one pays any attention to her" (107). It is Elena's particular charm to laugh goodhumoredly when making a withering observation about herself. Thus she laughs cheerfully when the man throws her out of his room. She caricatures herself sitting in the hall scribbling on the papers she "dragged everywhere, wherever she went" (105).

The event that climaxes the story is a non-event. Elena is waiting in the hall to catch a last glimpse of her ex-lover as he leaves. When he opens the door, however, a wind blows her pile of papers off the little table in the corner where she is sitting, and she is on her knees picking them up as he walks out. Because she missed this chance to see him, "her whole day was ruined" (109). The intense impact of such a minor event is in itself an ironic satirization of Elena's state of "love," as well as a tribute to Nakos's effectiveness in rendering Elena's perspective.

The second story about Elena, "Spring Invitation," is a more typical Nakos story in that it creates one mood that is suddenly jolted into another. The beginning creates a feeling of euphoria: Elena has at last recovered from the despair of being abandoned by her lover. She goes for a walk in the National Garden, which has the feel of an enchanted land, like the home of the Chinese couple in "Maternity." Elena enjoys spring and the attention of the young men in the park as if she were reborn. But when she leaves the park, the spell is broken. She meets her ex-lover's sister on her way to buy medicine for him. The realization that the man she loves is sick and she cannot go to him plunges Elena once more into her emotional hell. Whether the contrast is from despair to salvation, as in "Maternity," or from euphoria to despair, as in "Spring Invitation," Nakos is adept at portraying extreme swings of emotion.

Another story, "O Pateras" [The Father], is characterized by a similar rhythm. (This story is published in English as "The Rescue Party.") One of Nakos's best stories, it is told in the first person by a child who, together with her little brother, is taken each week to visit her father in an insane asylum.[6] Since she can see nothing wrong with him, she believes, with childlike passion, his contention that he has been unjustly committed by her mother. During one Sunday visit the father asks his children to come secretly to free him so that they can travel the world together. The little girl eagerly agrees to enact the oedipal fantasy, and she and her brother make careful preparations. They manage, with great travail, to make their way alone to the asylum. After hours of waiting outside the gates, they are rewarded with the horrific view of their father as a true madman having an insane fit, restrained by doctors and nurses.

"Thanasimi Voutia" [Fatal Plunge] portrays a situation rather than an event, and, even more unusual for Nakos, it is told from the point of view of a man and yields an extremely negative portrait of a woman, his wife.[7] It seems, in fact, like a spiteful fantasy imagined by Elena, the heroine of "Love," projecting disastrous results for her ex-lover if he marries his new woman instead of her. The protagonist of "Fatal Plunge"[8] realizes, a week after his wedding, that he has made a dreadful mistake in marrying a vulgar woman. He recalls with longing and regret the innocent and faithful virgin he rejected. He is trapped. The story merely presents his trap, ending, not with a striking event, but with a chilling extended image: the forlorn man sitting nightly in the railroad station watching trains pull out which cannot take him away from his wife. He must at last return home and slip into bed beside the fat, dirty body of his wife, listening to the train's far-off whistle.

One other story that stands out as atypical, "Tholi Istoria" [A Murky Story], consists of a mounting series of strange events and creates, in the process, a powerful and disturbing supernatural atmosphere. The story is reminiscent of Poe; it therefore may not be irrelevant that Nakos was, at about the time she wrote the story, writing a biography of Edgar Allan Poe and translating his stories for *Akropolis*.

The narrator of "A Murky Story" is a woman who meets a former fellow student, a mysterious, macabre, haunted sort of man who has lost those closest to him through death. It is clear that he personifies death, and the woman senses this, feeling badly shaken by the encounter. The man asks her to accompany him to the cemetery the next day. There they are separated by a funeral procession. After a frightening, desperate struggle to reach him, she finds him in front of a gravestone bearing his own name. The narrator later learns from the man's relatives that he died years before.

Aside from its unique tone of darkness and terror, this story is Nakos's only work in which there is a striking discrepancy between the protagonist's perception of reality and the reader's. There is an intriguing innuendo in the narrator's remark near the end, "They say all this to make my condition worse." What condition? How worse? The paranoia continues: "I'm sure of a lot of other things too, which might seem strange. It's better that I remain silent about them. Yes, for those who know strange stories like these, it's much better to remain silent" (98). Such tantalizing hidden meaning is not characteristic of Nakos's style, although it is not incongruent with her own interest in the occult.

The stories discussed thus far predate Nakos's first novel or were written during roughly the same period, just before World War II. They are most effective in introducing the point of view of a single character and in re-creating the intense emotional states experienced by her or him. The typical scheme involves establishing the situation with its attendant atmosphere and then, just before the end, introducing a startling event which brings about a sudden shift in mood. As has been seen, the stories exhibit themes and techniques that are later developed in Nakos's novels.

After the publication of *The Lost* (1935), Nakos wrote almost no stories for many years,[9] except for those written during World War II and later gathered under the title *The Children's Hell*. The seventeen stories in this collection are among her best and, until *The Lost* was serialized on Greek television in 1979, were her best-known work.

The Children's Hell

In keeping with her belief that art should be of use, Lilika Nakos considers *The Children's Hell* her most important book. She dedicated it "to the memory of the children who were mowed down by hunger in Greece during the winter of 41-42." A few of these children were brought to the Rizarion Seminary, converted into a makeshift hospital, where Nakos was a volunteer nurse for three grueling years during the German Occupation. Nakos tells that one day, as she passed a bed packed with five or six skeleton-thin creatures, a wasted arm reached out to tug her white apron. "They tell me you're a writer," the starving boy said. "Why don't you write about us, so people will know?" And that is what Nakos did.

The stories, smuggled out of Greece in the bosom of a foreign nurse, were immediately translated into French and printed in Switzerland, where they brought to world attention the famine in Greece, and as a result the International Red Cross began sending milk. The stories were published in Greek in Alexandria in 1944, and in French under the title *L'Enfer des Gosses* in Lausanne in 1946. In the same year *The Children's Inferno: Stories of the Great Famine in Greece* appeared in the United States, translated from the French, making this Nakos's only book available in English.[10] After the war, the stories were published in Greece in magazines and as a volume in 1959 and 1971.

Each story focuses on a single child, mostly *alitopaida,* vagrant-kids, whose parents have died or who have left their ruined homes to scrounge for bits of food by begging; by flopping in the street to feign dying in order to arouse the extra pity needed to earn them a crust; by stealing what little there was to be stolen; or by fighting equally ravenous dogs for the right to pick through garbage. The young protagonists are mostly boys; perhaps the little girls starved quietly at home while their brothers took to the streets and thus found their way to the hospital where Nakos could hear their stories and write them down. She captures the face of hunger that makes all the children look like little monkeys, sprouting a soft white down on their cheeks, and the feel of hunger that swells their throats so that they cannot swallow food when they find it.

Most of the stories are narrated by a nurse at the children's hospital, a "sister" of the Red Cross. On one level, the narrator is Nakos, undisguised, for she talks about her previous work at the newspaper and as a teacher as well as her years abroad; in several stories the children address her as "Mrs. Nakos." But the narrator generally recedes, leaving the children to tell their own stories to the nurse, or each other, or letting the head nurse tell them to the doctor.

The stories of *The Children's Hell* are about how people deal with maddening hunger which inexorably unhinges the structure of their lives. Children are the mirror through which the horror is reflected and refracted, as they struggle to maintain their humanity in an inhuman environment, trying to make sense of the senseless world adults are wrecking around them, finding ways to continue to live in the unlivable city of Athens.

Love among Ruins

Many of the children portrayed in these stories center their lives on love for someone or something: a baby sister ("Love"), a foreign soldier ("The Englishman," "Giovanni"), or an animal ("The Cat," "Buddies," "So That's How Our Life Is"). Their love is passionate and motivates small acts of vast heroism.

In "O Eglezos" [The Englishman] a child named Vasilakis and his friend save the life of a wounded British soldier named Harry, and hide him in their home: a cave near the Akropolis. The three share what food they find and sleep close together for warmth. When the Englishman is captured, Vasilakis jumps onto the

German truck to throw him a piece of dry bread. A German soldier kicks him off, breaking his leg. As the leg refuses to heal, Vasilakis' only regret is that when the English return, and he runs to greet his friend, Harry won't recognize him in his crippled, limping state.

Another story concerns a friendship between two Greek boys and an Italian soldier whom they call "Tzovanni" [Giovanni], but it is the soldier who brings the boys food. Giovanni is captured when the Germans turn against the Italians, rounding them up and marching them off. The boy Spiros marches beside his Italian, carrying his bag and supporting him. The German guard is angered by this show of affection and swings his rifle at "Giovanni," but Spiros springs to take the blow. Enraged, the German sends the boy sprawling and stamps on him to make sure he stays down in a pool of blood.

Nikos Atzamis in "Syntrofoi" [Buddies] must be carted to the hospital because his legs are covered with the open wounds of vitamin deficiency, yet he finds strength to sneak out rather than separate from the dog waiting for him at the door. When the dog is killed by a car, Nikos carries the corpse in his arms to bury him, vowing to sleep on the grave every night.

The hero of another story, Kostas, also used to sleep with his pet, "To Gati" [The Cat], until his hunger-crazed mother and older half-brother butcher and eat it. The grim ritual takes place in the middle of the night; the older boy drags the cat to the wash-hut, where it eludes him like a possessed creature. Finally he brings the dead cat to his mother who cooks it as if in a trance, dazed by hunger and by the moon whose eery light drips through the skylight. The smell of cooking meat dizzies them and awakens the smallest children who creep into the kitchen to discover the silent feast, the older boy licking the plate, his fingers, the pan. Kostas wakes screaming in his bed, hearing the shrieks of his beloved cat long after she has been eaten. The frightful drama continues as the story ends, for the feverish child hallucinates, as he caresses the visiting nurse's hand:

"Kitty! My little kitty!... You came back to me?... And I thought they killed you and something inside me cracked, here! Welcome back, kitty, little kitty. Welcome back!" And he stroked the nurse's hand with his burning palm... (73)

The child is the conscience of his race, unable to accept what his family has become.

The same is true of little Minas in "Etsi Loipon Einai I Zoi Mas" [So That's How Our Life Is].[11] When his mother tells how the family finally sold their beloved donkey to the butcher, tears fall from his eyes, but they are "silent tears, strange for a child, without weeping or sobbing." He opens his lips to speak only once before he also dies, to ask, "So that's how life is?" Minas has been struck dumb by the realization that "for a piece of bread or a little gold, people can sell to the butcher what is most dear to them in the world" (218).

Some of the children find love by banding together in a kind of family, since their own families have died, fallen apart, or sent them to Athens from a starving island. One of the best stories, and the longest, "Karderina,"[12] portrays a pack of boys who have made their home in an abandoned shelter, with "the Arab" as their leader. This story is unusual for Nakos because its impact does not derive from plot. It is simply a portrait of the gang, focusing on their leader, and the interaction among its members as well as between them and Karderina, a young girl who sings in the subway to support herself and her old aunt. The story climaxes when the Arab confesses to Karderina that he is dying: as he watched the grim wagon creeking through the streets piled with the day's corpses, an arm dangled out the back, swinging and beckoning him to join them. Karderina sings him a mournful song to a cypress tree: "Take me with you." Karderina's song, her company, and her love ease the Arab's way to death. The gang's shelter is on the *iero odo,* the Holy Road along which ancient pilgrims traveled to Eleusis, whose mysteries were associated with an underworld cult. The story is a procession as the Arab journeys on the figurative road to death.

Innocent Visions

Manolis in the story "To Perivoli tou Theou" [God's Garden] paves his own way down the road to death by creating elaborate fantasies of a happier world. When his little brother dies because Manolis has collapsed and can no longer bring him food, he dreams that his brother is happy in "God's Garden." Stricken by a measles epidemic that leaves few survivors in the children's ward, Manolis joins his brother in the happier garden. Despotis in "To Mati tou Theou" [The Eye of God] is also a little boy with a vision, but his is a nightmare of a huge eye crying enormous tears over what it sees in the world. The next day, remembering his mother's explanation that the eye painted in the church dome is the eye of God, Despotis climbs up to the top of the church and covers the eye to protect God from the dreadful sight of the great famine.

In reality, no one can be spared this sight, least of all the children. The impact of some of the stories hinges on the children's simple acceptance of bizarre and unthinkable circumstances, as if they never expected life to be any different from this hell. "I Trelli" [The Madwoman], broken by the insufferable famine, is put in the hospital because the insane asylum is closed, all its inmates having starved to death. The only "medicine" that can calm her so she will eat is a daily beating from her husband, as if his is a wrath she can comprehend. The gentle husband forces himself to play this macabre role, leaving his little girl outside while he "gives Mommy her medicine." One day he breaks down, sobbing, and his little daughter asks simply, "Did you beat Mommy very hard today? Is that why you're crying?" (204)

Another story derives its impact from a different sort of shock. "Elenitsa" is strangely untouched by the ravages around her. While the other children in the hospital groan and cry, she lies placid, smiling radiantly at anyone who passes. The head nurse, charmed by the angelic child, asks her what she wants, and the little girl pipes up, with absolute trust that her wish will be granted, "French fries!" The utter impossibility, the absurdity of the request reminds the nurses that there might exist in the world such a thing as fried potatoes. This effect is heightened by Elenitsa's use of the diminutive ending *itsa: "Patatitses tiganites,"* "little fried potatoes," as if they were a simple little thing, perhaps echoing a mother tenderly coaxing a child to eat up. The head nurse manages the miracle just before Elenitsa dies but not in time for her to raise the precious food to her mouth; the nurse pries the little fingers open so that Elenitsa may appear before God "without *patatitses*," with only "empty and crossed little hands."

The most horrific stories of *The Children's Hell* are the two about victims of the atrocities in Macedonia beside which the appalling starvation in Athens shrinks to insignificance. A strikingly beautiful fourteen-year-old girl ironically named Niki (Victory) is from "Macedonia," where rampaging Bulgarians slaughtered her family before her eyes, raped her, cut out her tongue, and lopped off her hands. She is placed in a tent pitched in the courtyard of the overcrowded hospital for a family of survivors from another Macedonian village, a family whose mother spends her time making tiny graves, while one of her little boys constructs miniature crosses to mark them. A German officer and a Bulgarian come to inspect the hospital. The German remarks scornfully that in Germany no tent would ever be permitted on hospital grounds. Pushed beyond fury, the head nurse offers calmly but insistently to take him to the tent. Once inside, the German fixes his eyes upon Niki, wrapped in her cape.

He stood with admiration before this lovely living statue who looked at him with frightened eyes. He smiled to her and held out his hand.
    The girl drew back, frightened, uttering an inarticulate cry. With this sudden movement, her mutilated stumps appeared!

The officers leave immediately without a word.

The moment they left, however, something unexpected happened. The madwoman rose and followed him, holding in her hands a box in which she had built a little tomb decorated with a tiny wooden cross. Her little lame son came up behind her with his crutches, followed by the other little cripples. We all looked on in amazement at this strange procession. The little cripple's crutches were heard, tock-tock, on the tiles of the path in the yard. (210)

A Message of Forgiveness

The hospital inspection is one of the few occasions when the enemy appears. Nakos chronicles and dramatizes the suffering of the Greeks without blaming. This combination of horror portrayed with a generous spirit toward all people is seen most clearly in "To Amartima tis Yiayias" [The Grandmother's Sin]. An old woman and her two grandchildren are the only survivors from their Macedonian village. Now safe in the Athens hospital, the terror-stricken children relive the Bulgarian attack, their eyes blackened with fright, as the sister screams and her little brother silently clutches at her with the stumps of his arms. In another room their dying grandmother wishes to confess. Her only sin is that she cannot hate the Bulgarians for what they have done. She can't help feeling pity for them as well.

A similar message of forgiveness emerges in "Synayermos" [Air Raid], in which three children, awakened during the night by sirens, discuss the war. A small boy from Piraeus asks the unanswerable question, "Why do people kill each other?" One little patient suggests, "It's God's will," to which the young cynic replies scornfully, "What does God have to do with it?" Another says, "It's fate." This is no more satisfying to the questioner: "What does 'fate' mean?" Finally he offers his own answer: "The big governments want to divide up the earth between them . . ." (120). The boys also tackle the question of manliness. They all boast that they never scramble into shelters when the alarms sound. "That's for women!" one of them announces (121). At the end, a child named Iorgos, enraged to hear that the other two do not hate the Germans and the Italians, fumes, "And you think you're men?!" The wise little Piraeus boy's retort is echoed in the last line of the story: "A man is someone who's not afraid of anything... And if he feels like it, he isn't afraid to say what he thinks... And if he feels like loving all people, he isn't afraid to say so! That's what it means to be a man—not just cursing and telling people to go to hell!" (124)

Thus the children try to come to terms with the devastation around them. Hardly remembering any other life, some adapt to it more easily than the adults and become the supporters of their helpless families, like Karderina, Manolis in "God's Garden," and Iorgos in "Love." The most successful child in this respect is Epaminondas in "Athanati Ratsa" [Immortal Race], who becomes a symbol of Greece's refusal to be crushed. For Epaminondas (his name is reminiscent of the Greek verb *epimeno*, to insist or endure), the hospital is only a temporary waystation. "Hey, I want to live!..." he insists. "We should all live! Just like that, for spite!... Since they're all bent on killing us with hunger, we will live! We won't give them the satisfaction!" (172) The narrator/nurse marvels at the boy's determination and resourcefulness; after he leaves the hospital she meets him again: as a "prosperous" merchant, buying and selling used goods from a cart, trading with skill and of course guile. There is an underlying irony, an agony perhaps, as she sees the little hero masterfully manipulate a customer to despair in order to prime her for a sale, even though in the end he insists that he hasn't cheated her.

In narrating these stories, Nakos adopts a Voltairian arch-innocent persona who looks uncritically at everyone. She uses the almost stupidly innocent stance as a foil to reflect what may be the reader's not-so-thoughtful view, or to evoke a revelation from a character. For example, in "Love," the nurse has been visiting Iorgos's house and has heard his mother's incredulous pride that Iorgos has been keeping his baby sister alive by occasionally—miraculously!—bringing her milk. So when the nurse later sees the little boy in a field, looking around guiltily as he approaches a she-donkey with a pail, she must certainly know the answer to her question "Hey, Iorgos!... Is the animal yours?" But her assumed naiveté gives Iorgos the chance to explain that it had been theirs, until his father sold it (62). Similarly, in "God's Garden," after Manolis learns that his little brother has starved to death because Manolis has been in the hospital, he wakes up the next morning smiling happily. The narrator thinks, "That's children for you! Luckily for them, they immediately forget anything bad that happens to them..." She can then chide herself and any thick-skinned readers: "But I was fooled." Manolis is happy because he has dreamed that his little brother is happy at last in God's Garden.

The first-person narrative allows Nakos to emphasize the conclusion to be drawn from a story, for example by pointing out that Epaminondas represents the tenacity of the Greek race, or by repeating the little boy's philosophy that one should not be afraid to love all people. This didactic bent is perhaps most appropriate to *The Children's Hell*, which is literature as political action and social statement, an act of resistance. The book remains, for all time, a document of the great famine in Greece during the German Occupation.

After the war, Nakos, exhausted and ill as a result of her own great suffering and starvation during the Occupation, an ordeal she chose not to write about, preferring to portray the suffering of others, made her way to Switzerland where she lectured tirelessly on the plight of the Greek children, continuing in person the campaign that she had initiated by sending her stories ahead.

Chapter Three
Cruel Fatherland: *The Deflowered One*

The Greek novel was still in its infancy when *I Xepartheni* [The Deflowered One] hit the Greek literary scene in 1932.[1] The critic C. Dimaras called it "a new beginning in our literature,"[2] and the poet Kostis Palamas commented, "rarely has a book moved me so deeply."[3] Nakos wrote *Le Livre de Mon Pierrot* in French while she was living in Paris; it won first prize in an international story contest sponsored by the newspaper *Le Petit Parisien* in 1928. On her return to Greece in 1930, she rewrote the novella in Greek, but it was not she who clapped on the sensational Greek title. "I didn't even know the word," she remarked to me. Unfortunately, the title *The Deflowered One* has stuck and has been kept through all reprintings.

The suggestive Greek title, and a lurid paper cover showing a sexy woman with her red blouse falling off one shoulder, exploited the revolutionary nature of Nakos's subject. The novella recounts the experiences and thoughts of a young woman who is secretly raising an illegitimate child. No less startling was Nakos's use of conversational demotic to render the first-person narrative. Moreover, the entire novella is a powerful social critique, depicting the difficulties faced by a working woman and the callousness of the upper class.

The Story

The Deflowered One is narrated by Katina Tade[4] who, like Nakos and other of her heroines, is the daughter of upper-class parents who do not get along with each other. Katina is a hard-working, good-humoredly ironic young woman, a typical Nakos heroine who narrates events with simplistic innocence. Katina left her home in Greece for Paris at eighteen, but when she heard that her father was sick in Austria, she rushed to his side, nursed him to health, and then returned with him to Greece.

Back in Athens, Katina met and fell in love with a young Frenchman named Michel who eventually returned to France, leaving Katina pregnant. When the novella begins, Katina is supporting her son Petros by working at a newspaper as a translator (she later takes on a second job, drawing sketches for a store). The child Petros lives with Mrs. Kontylo, a saintly old woman from the island of Hydra who was Katina's nursemaid and her father's before her.[5] Katina leads a double life, having dinner with her parents at midday and spending evenings with Petros and Mrs. Kontylo, before returning to her own apartment near Lycabettos Hill.

When Katina's mother has an accident and thinks she may die, she asks Katina to locate her children by a previous marriage, whom Katina has never met. Her half-sister Loukia turns out to be a cold and ambitious career woman and society wife, but her half-brother George is a fiery and good-hearted Communist who becomes Katina's friend. Another friend is a gentle doctor named Spanides who saves the baby Petros when he is ill and continues to visit Petros and Katina, as does a fatherly Dr. X., who was Katina's own doctor when she was a child.

Katina has one more devoted friend, a kind Frenchman named M. Tantel, who wants to marry her. She refuses him because she is devoted solely to Petros and the memory of Michel. Katina must fight off the advances of Alex, the evil brother of Dr. Spanides. Alex continually accosts Katina as she leaves Mrs. Kontylo's house late at night. In the end, he tells Katina's father about her illegitimate child and, at the father's behest, murders both Petros and Mrs. Kontylo. Katina runs to her father, intending to kill herself before his eyes, but he faints, and she begins to minister to him instead. When he revives, he tries to kiss her, but she runs away. Katina falls ill with grief and languishes for a time in a French hospital. When she recovers, she sails once more for Paris, to start a new life far from her harsh fatherland.

Cruel Father

The main force behind *The Deflowered One* derives from Katina's intense and ambivalent involvement with her father: a stingy, lascivious, and autocratic man. Throughout the book this man is referred to as Katina's *patrios*, or "stepfather." However, there can be no question that this character is the heroine's father, both from the details of the narrative and from the nature of the characters' interaction. Moreover, on three occasions the narrator apparently forgets the ruse and calls this man her "father," *pateras*. More basic are elements such as the fact that Katina tells of undergoing a test for congenital syphilis (George Ventiris argues in the introduction that she actually had it), and this is in keeping with the corrupt character of her *patrios* who she says "caught the most awful disease from a Polish countess" (14). Similarly, Katina recalls the brothers of a young servant who had been seduced by him, coming to the house when she was a child and spitting on her, calling her "dirty seed of your father" (35). Finally, Katina is said to have inherited his violent temper (18). Moreover, her mother has two children by a former marriage who were raised by their father, and the present husband is her second and only other one. So no one but he can be Katina's father. Therefore, I will refer to this man as the father, a policy that has been adopted by other critics without explanation.

In response to the obvious question of why Nakos bothered to adopt the transparent veil of *patrios* at all, reference need simply be made to her father's prominence and the fact that Greek readers tended to view her fiction as autobiography. When I asked her directly, she answered: "So as not to say that it was my father."

In the novella, when Katina told Mrs. Kontylo of her pregnancy, the wise old woman said, "It's not your fault... Let the blame fall on your father who never wanted to let you get married" (22). Indeed, although the main action concerns the child Petros, Katina's main preoccupation is keeping his existence secret from her father. As the one responsible for the child's death at the end, the father is the story's principal villain.

The father is also associated with Greece, a fatherland that is seen as cruel and stingy to its children. Katina's psychological development in the novella constitutes her working free of emotional involvement with her father, so that at the end she has achieved sufficient distance not to care what happened to him. Simultaneously, she works free of Greece and sails for France again at the end.

A Voyage into the Past

The structure of *The Deflowered One* follows a pattern that is found in all Nakos's novels. At two points in the work, once in the middle and once just before the end, events reach a low ebb and the protagonist experiences an emotional nadir. This plunge, however, is immediately followed by a sharp upsurge. This structure is particularly appropriate to Nakos's skill in portraying extremes of emotion and to her preference for optimistic, hopeful endings.

In *The Deflowered One* Katina descends into psychological depths in the form of semi-conscious states. The first such episode, occurring midway through the work, consists of her recollection of undergoing a spinal tap in Zurich, Switzerland, to determine whether she had congenital syphilis and could therefore never have a child. The second emotional "descent" is represented by her stay in the French hospital after her collapse following the murder of Petros and his nursemaid.

Ostensibly, the first "descent" episode is a flashback, while the second is part of the narrative proper; that is, in the middle of her narrative, Katina lies on her bed and daydreams about the previous experience of the spinal tap, and she recalls that the results were negative. She subsequently returned to Greece and eventually gave birth to Petros.

Another interpretation is suggested by George Ventiris' discussion, in his introduction, of the symbolic nature of Petros's life and death.

Only reference to symbol actually explains the tragedy of the remote house in Plaka. The longing of the young woman who wants to become a mother and cannot because the doctor whispered something in her ear: the instinct of motherhood which is cut off at the roots by the blind influences of her forebears, that's what kills Peter.

Extending this interpretation, one can surmise that the spinal tap in Switzerland revealed that Katina had indeed inherited syphilis from her father and therefore could not have a baby. The entire novella, then, can be seen to represent her fantasy of having the child she longs for. Katina's recollection of the spinal tap experience recounts a drug-induced series of visions followed by an interminable period of emotional anguish, including recollections of Greece. The section ends with Katina's comment, "It's true, then, as the peasants tell us, that when a person dies, their soul returns to the places where they suffered most in the earthly world" (60).

If the news that she cannot have a child is a death to Katina, as indeed she says, "To condemn a woman to never having a child is like killing her life itself inside her" (57), then perhaps Katina's soul returns to the place where she suffered most: as a child in Greece, rejected by her parents who were engrossed in their own endless battles. Thus when she says, "Lying in bed, with my eyes closed, I relive the past," there are two possible levels of significance. On the obvious level, she is on the bed in Athens, reliving the earlier experience in Switzerland. From the second perspective, she may be lying on her bed in Switzerland reliving and imagining experiences in Athens, surrounding her father and the dream of a baby which he has destroyed.

There is a clear connection between Katina's illness in Switzerland and her present state. She recalls, "It was the same season, more or less" (57). In Zurich she remembered "the dust-covered pine trees in the Zappeion, and the March weather of Athens" (59)—the same March season which figures significantly in the events of this story.

Pagan Passion

The Deflowered One is a passion play, a reenactment of the Easter pageant. The two-dimensional characters are revealed in a patchwork of unfolding action and flashbacks, culminating in the denouement which takes place during "the Great Week," the week before Easter. The child Petros is killed, like Christ, on that Thursday and buried on Friday, the same day that Katina from her window overlooking the city watches the "river of fire"—the traditional orthodox ceremony in which a candle-bearing procession follows the *epitaphios*, Christ's bier, through the streets of Athens.

The Christian allegory dovetails with pagan fertility ritual. The events of the novella take place in March, carnival season, and the streets are full of masqueraders. Little Petros wears a *martios*, a bracelet of gold and red threads which Greek peasants believe will protect him from the March sun, like a primitive talisman. The spirit of the Dionysian season touches Katina herself: she is overcome by a physical longing for a young man in her office, even for strange men in the street. The supernatural atmosphere is heightened by numerous elements: Katina's prescient dreams, her father's reputed "evil eye," and the incense with which Mrs. Kontylo continually fumigates the house. The backdrop for the events is the teeming Eastern-style market, as Katina makes her way home alone from visiting her son at Mrs. Kontylo's house through the narrow crooked streets of the old section of Plaka.

In this setting the sacrificial ritual is foreshadowed:

They still slaughter the lambs there and make *kokoretsi*.[6] The air smells of smoke and it would whet your appetite, if you didn't see the blood running down the streets of the big market. (27)

Petros's death is associated with the death of Christ, first, because of the timing of his death in the Easter pageant. In addition, Katina comments that "for a hundred drachmas Alex would betray even Christ" (94), and indeed it is Alex, the bad brother of her friend Dr. Spanides, who in the end betrays Petros.

If Petros's murder is the crucifixion, what then is the resurrection? This question inspires a closer look at Katina's love for her son Petros and his father Michel. Katina has been living in the hope of an impending visit by Michel to Athens. On Easter Sunday she receives a letter from him informing her that he has married an American named Mabel and will not come to see her. Thus Katina permanently loses Michel at the same time that she loses his son. She is inconsolable. But Michel's letter comes on Easter Sunday, the day of the resurrection. Observed in this light, Petros's death and Michel's remarriage can be seen finally to free Katina from her grueling life in Greece.

Greek critics have made much of Katina's great love for her son, holding it up as the virtue that redeems the unwed mother's sin. Despite its sentimentality, this interpretation may be satisfying on one level, and it is consonant with Katina's own point of view. From another perspective, however, Katina's love for Petros is a caricature of maternal devotion, an orgy of self-sacrifice.

Petros is a spoiled brat. If his mother forgets to bring him a present one day, he sulks, "Oh, bad Mommy who forgot her Petros...." Seeing an expensive ball in a store window, he insists on having it, even though his mother cannot afford it. Katina buys Petros the ball, thinking, "So I won't eat one evening..."! Petros pulls her hair and won't let her talk to anyone else; he won't even let her mind travel. He "pulls her from her dreams" when she is recalling the Zurich clinic experience. The child is destructive:

He climbs into bed next to me. He is holding a broken toy, and he tells me how he managed to destroy it. He's very proud of this. Mrs. Kontylo has finished her prayer. She comes with the censer to spread incense around us. Petros sneezes: Nanny get angry and calls him "a little Frank." (61)

The all-loving nursemaid is frightened by the sacrilegious irreverence which she attributes to his French paternity.

Katina exhausts herself at two jobs in order to support Petros. Furthermore, her involvement with him prevents her from forming any relationship with another man (28).

Even Katina herself has occasional insight into the ambivalent joys of motherhood:

> Is that what they call "Motherhood"? Is it this uneasy love, all agony which I feel for my Petros? Everywhere, wherever I am, my thoughts are elsewhere. With my child. I tremble when it's cold. When he goes out, lest he fall. If he eats custard, that it might spoil his stomach. A heap of "ifs" drive me mad. (29)

And again, "My God, I have such love for this child, sometimes I'm afraid I'll lose my mind" (46).

Certainly, this is not to say that Katina consciously regrets having Petros, nor that she sees her love for him in a negative light. She adores him, as she adored his father Michel. Yet it is this love that keeps her at the killing work of two jobs in the Greece reverberating with her parents' voices. The resurrection, then, at the end of the novella, is Katina's, as she escapes the ghosts of her past: realistically, the demands of her child and the memory of her ex-lover Michel, and symbolically the devastating spirits of her ill-fated parents.

The Peasant, the Loving Mother

Katina's parents represent the negative associations of her childhood in Greece. In contrast, Mrs. Kontylo, an island-born peasant, is a romantic ideal of Greece and the Greek people much as Ireland is represented as an old woman in Irish literature. Mrs. Kontylo is the incarnation of perfect goodness and love. She is also associated with the Holy Mother, seated among the icons in her house which "looks like a church": "A red candle burns night and day before the icons. It always smells of incense. The walls are pure white" (22).

Moreover, Nakos depicts the place where Mrs. Kontylo lives as an otherworld nestled in the streets of the old section of Athens: "Around it is a great yard with trees. And it seems as if she lives apart from the world" (22). At carnival time, when the events of the story begin, the masqueraders in the streets are like strange spirits calling out to Katina, trying to catch her.

The house in Plaka where the old nursemaid lives with Peter is paradise, while the real world is hell. To travel between these worlds, Katina crosses a strange threshold:

> There's the well, over there, whose water one must never bend to see at night. A spirit lives in it, the people say. And if you scare it, it can harm you. On the other side is the tank and that big fig tree. I turn left into the little street that's always full of washwater, and I find myself on Amalias Avenue. (31)

Both the haunted well and the fig tree are images from Greek folklore that recur in Nakos's work. Peasants in Greece believe wells to be the homes of spirits, and they believe that the devil appears under fig trees.[7] In the description of the street that Katina crosses when leaving Mrs. Kontylo's house, the well spirit seems to be guarding the entrance to the underworld, for the fig tree—the devil's haunt—is on the other side. Furthermore, the washwater running through the street is like the River Styx that must be crossed in order to get to Hades, the underworld in Greek mythology.

When Katina is in Mrs. Kontylo's house she is perfectly happy, and only idealized characters are permitted to enter there: the good doctors, Katina's friend M. Tantel, and her half-brother George.

The Good Doctors and Other Characters

If Mrs. Kontylo is an idealized mother figure, there is also an idealized father figure: Doctor X., who regularly visits Katina and Petros.[8] He is "the same age as my father." In true Freudian fashion Katina says he is "the first man I think I loved, at age ten." She goes on:

> I liked to feel him near me, when he bent over my bed to see what was wrong with me. When we had him over for dinner, for Mister X, and

only for him, I put on my blue skirt with the white piqué. I wanted him to like me, and I was jealous when he talked to anyone else. Whatever medicine he gave me, I took without complaining. The strangest part is that now I've grown up, the men I like must always be like him, look like him. Michel, for example, reminds me of him. He has the long dark face, the thin lips. Only in his expression he doesn't resemble him. (49)

Dr. X. takes a paternal interest in Katina and her son, as her own father does not.

Similarly, the young Dr. Spanides plays the role of an idealized father to Petros. He is responsible for the boy's life, since he saves him from a severe fever. In gratitude Katina presents him with the engagement ring Michel had given her. Dr. Spanides lives in Plaka near Mrs. Kontylo, and after Katina moves in with her, they all eat together daily like a family: mother, son, "father," and nursemaid.

Both doctors are idealized male figures: protective, good, and sexless. The antithesis, all that Katina finds repulsive in men, is embodied in Dr. Spanides' evil brother Alex. (The technique of embodying opposites in a pair of siblings is seen in many later Nakos works as well.) Like the devil, Alex is seen under a fig tree in the garden. That Alex represents an aspect of Katina's father is most obvious because although it is he who murders Petros and Mrs. Kontylo, yet he is regarded simply as the father's agent.

In keeping with the interpretation that *The Deflowered One* is a fantasized drama enacted by characters from Katina's past, Alex is the same man who molested her when she was six or seven. Katina recalls this scene in the present tense, a technique Nakos often employs to create immediacy and to heighten emotional impact.

"Come here, my little one," he goes, "and I'll give you candy." My first impulse is to leave. But then again, my mother always says I have to be polite to everyone... So I go up to him. I'm afraid, I want to leave. But he squeezes me so tight, I don't have the strength to move. I want to cry. But he keeps rubbing himself against me, panting...

A great repulsion seizes me... I can't stand it—I shout... Steps are heard in the row of trees. Then he lets me go and disappears among the trees. I return running to Mrs. Kontylo and tell her everything. She turns deep red with anger. She grabs an umbrella and runs to find him. But Alex has disappeared. Only on my little piqué skirt I see a liquid sticking to it like gum. (54)

Alex represents the negative side of men, associated with the aspects of Katina's father which she hates, while the doctors embody a paternal ideal. Katina's oedipal attachment to her father is clear. She often takes her mother's place in accompanying her father to social functions, and it is she who nurses him when he is sick. She is happy when she sees him (26), despite her avowed hatred of him. However, Katina cannot act on her positive feelings for him. On the few occasions when he shows affection for her, she is paralyzed and cannot respond.

Katina's attraction to her father is acted upon by the character named Vartoui: a sensual, belly-dancing, fortune-telling Jewish woman of the same age as Katina whom her father sets up in the basement of his house as a live-in mistress. Vartoui advises Katina to be coquettish with her father in order to get money from him. She suggests Katina tell him, as Vartoui herself does, "My precious Daddy, I love you so much!" (68). Katina, however, cannot play this sexual game.

When the father is enraged at Vartoui for having a young boyfriend, his fury is reminiscent of his attitude toward his daughter. Katina comments early in her narrative that "this honorable man never stopped running to bordellos," yet "he would prefer to have me die a thousand deaths rather than learn I had a lover" (15).

If Vartoui represents one aspect of Katina's impulses, Katina's half-sister Loukia represents another. Loukia is a successful career woman and wife, the pride of her mother because she has "a place in society." Just as Katina goes to Vartoui's room and listens to her rail against men without taking her advice about how to exploit them, so she goes to Loukia's dinner party and observes Athenian high society but remains apart from it.

Women and Other Victims

Nakos's novels are often characterized by a stark distinction between good and bad people. In *The Deflowered One* this duality is especially clear-cut for male characters. Alex and the father are bad; the doctors, Katina's friend M. Tantel, and her half-brother George are good. The women, however, are somewhat more complex. Only the old peasant Mrs. Kontylo is clearly idealized. The mother, although weak and superficial, is good-natured, and she earns the reader's sympathy when she is victimized by her husband. The mistress Vartoui exploits the father because she has no other means of support, but she too is a good person, as even Katina's mother admits. The half-sister Loukia is understandably unrelenting toward her mother who abandoned her to marry Katina's father, but she is kind to Katina. All the women's shortcomings are comprehensible and forgivable because they are victims.

The mother, at the same time that she is a victim as a woman, is also representative of the upper class which victimizes workers, as part of the social system which is depicted in the novella. Kosmas Politis, one of the foremost novelists of the Generation of the Thirties, writing in *Sosialistiki Zoi* [Socialist Life], takes Nakos to task for blaming the father for Katina's fate.[9] According to him, society is at fault. Politis mistakenly confuses Nakos the writer with Katina the protagonist. Katina may blame her father for everything, but Nakos portrays the father as representative of the entrenched powers of the social and political system. His status in society, and the power he exercises through control of the purse strings, identify him as such, and there is little equivocation about Nakos's judgment of him in this regard. He is hopelessly dissolute, and his demeanor is so sinister that "passersby in the street turn to look at him. No one would want to have anything to do with him" (25). He is so stingy that his wife suffers from hunger, and their dog starves to death!

The mother, in turn, represents the indolent bourgeoisie, living off the father and legitimizing his power by submitting to it. Her corrupt values lead her to adore her uncaring successful daughter Loukia who refuses to have anything to do with her, and to scorn the Communist son who loves and wants to help her. Katina describes her parents' relationship with wry humor: "All in all everything is going well. My parents continue to hate each other without however being able to separate" (45). The mutually destructive embrace of their marriage mirrors the vicious social system which they represent.

The socialist critic, Politis, concludes, despite his criticism, that Nakos is "with us" because she loves the *laos,* the people. Indeed, Katina's scorn for her mother contrasts with her love for her nursemaid, Mrs. Kontylo, whom Politis calls, with justification, the true heroine. Katina idealizes her peasant nursemaid: "She makes other people's pain her own. Most peasants are like that. They have great sympathy. While Mother, if you tell her such things, cuts you off. 'Oh, now you're exaggerating.' She's very bourgeois. Her life has always been mediocre. Without great sorrow and with meaningless joys" (57). Elsewhere Katina comments, "But they're the same everywhere, the middle and upper classes: shallow, superficial" (17).

In its entirety *The Deflowered One* is a commentary on the position of the worker, and particularly the working woman, in Greece. Katina is in a double bind. She is forced to work and is then looked down on for working. Moreover, Katina's suffering as a result of her poverty, her exhaustion from sitting up nights working at a second job, her panic of losing her income and having no way to feed her child, are all eloquent comments on the workers' difficult lot.

Katina's Communist half-brother George is a good character, one of the privileged few who are admitted to the dreamworld of Mrs. Kontylo's house. Although Katina adopts an arch-innocent stance toward George's political diatribes, claiming not to understand most of what he says, she admits to understanding at least this: "The people are hungry, and without doubt they can't stand the rich. They don't want philosophy. And as things progress, matters get worse." But she stops short of revolutionary solutions. Rather, she feels, "Only work will save us. Each one should eat by his own sweat." George is a living refutation of the accusation voiced at Loukia's party that Communists are lazy, or, as Kontylo's priest tells her, antichrists. Yet M. Tantel's rebuttal of George's party line is convincing: "The Greek is a merchant. He has it in his blood" (76). *The Deflowered One* portrays and decries economic injustice and social hypocrisy but, although it hails George's good intentions, it clearly does not endorse his Communist solution. Nakos's first major work, *The Deflowered One* establishes a pattern that reappears in later works: the portrayal of a woman's personal struggle set against and largely created by social forces, straightforwardly narrated in lyrical demotic language which reflects and re-creates the heroine's innocence. This novella is a midpoint between the short stories that Nakos wrote before and the full-length novels she wrote after. It is a bit more sentimental and also more allegorical than the works that follow, and it affords one of Nakos's bleaker portraits of life in Greece. Nonetheless, the seed of Nakos's later romanticization of Greece is seen in the character Mrs. Kontylo.

Chapter Four
The Holy Virgin in Hell: *The Lost*

In 1934 Lilika Nakos was working at three jobs: mornings she taught at the Eighth Boys' High School in Patisia; evenings she wrote for the newspaper *Akropolis;* weekends she directed, wrote plays, and trained assistants for the first puppet theater in Greece which she had established in the Zappeion park. In addition, she awoke every morning at 4 A.M. to steal a few hours to write her first long novel, *Oi Parastratimenoi,* literally, "those who have strayed from the straight path." I have adopted the English title, *The Lost,* following the critic Linos Politis.

Politis exclaims, "A great stir was caused by the publication of *The Lost* (1935)."[1] According to I. M. Panayiotopoulos, *"The Lost* represented a great step forward. I consider the book one of the most significant which the period between the wars has given us."[2] *The Lost* is the first book that Nakos wrote directly in Greek, and it was later translated into French and published in Paris as *Alexandra* and in Switzerland as *Les Devoyagees.* It is based upon Nakos's life as a young girl in pre-World War I Geneva.

The Lost is a first-person narrative, the *bildungsroman* of Alexandra Kastri, chronicling her early childhood in Greece and her young adulthood in Geneva. The elements of style that appeared in Nakos's stories and in her novella *The Deflowered One* are seen here, matured and developed. The simple demotic language flows easily and lyrically. Alexandra speaks openly about her most intimate experiences and emotions. The world she inhabits is dangerous and unjust. Like Katina in *The Deflowered One,* Alexandra is totally innocent, hurt by her dark environment and the thoughtlessness and cruelty of others, yet she is isolated from it and uncorrupted by it. Whereas the secondary characters in *The Deflowered One* are primarily symbolic and therefore flat, in *The Lost* Nakos creates a vivid and realistic gallery of secondary characters who form the background for Alexandra's personal struggles as well as the social environment that reflects or causes them. Central to the vision that emerges from the work is the searing poverty of some, juxtaposed with the carelessness and callousness of others. In this conflict the hope for "a better life," which is expressed by characters in all of Nakos's work, is subtly yet clearly represented by the efforts of a caring few expatriate Russian revolutionaries, as well as by an optimistic ending. While ostensibly a first-person narrative, the novel does not strictly maintain the first-person point of view but intersperses Alexandra's with the points of view of other characters.

The Story

When the novel opens, Alexandra, apparently about seven, is riding in a carriage with her godmother, with whom she is going to live. A beloved little sister has just died (one recalls here Nakos's early French story "Mort de Chrissi"), and her parents feared she would suffer physical harm at the hands of her sadistic brother Nikos. In answer to her godmother's question, the child snaps impetuously, "I'll never love you and I don't love my mother either!" But in fact she comes to love her godmother deeply. The two years she spends with her on her estate outside Athens become an idealized Paradise Lost which Alexandra later recalls with longing.

The godmother has long loved Alexandra's father, but he chose to marry Nitsa, Alexandra's mother, who in turn is passionately in love with her first cousin Sotiris (whom she could not marry because the Greek church forbids marriage between first cousins).[3] Sotiris is, in fact, the real father of Alexandra's older brother Nikos, and there are hints that this consanguinity is the cause of Nikos's crippled leg, if not his incorrigible character. When Nitsa, the mother, invites her cousin Sotiris to come and live with her, Alexandra's father, finding the prospect of a threesome intolerable, moves to Egypt.

When her mother takes Alexandra back from the godmother to live with her and Sotiris, the scene depicting the child's return feels rather like a vicious kidnapping, an impression justified by the atmosphere of agony and deprivation that awaits her in her mother's house, where the only love is Nitsa's crazed passion for Sotiris, plus some spillover from this to his child, Nikos, who continues to torment his sister mercilessly.

Sotiris is suddenly forced to flee the country because of fraudulent stock dealings, and Nitsa takes to her bed in despair. Alexandra becomes the effective though always unappreciated head of the household which is riddled with debts. The family is left in a house bare even of furniture which has been carried off by creditors. On the day when the last piece of bread has been eaten, a brief renascence occurs: the father returns, temporarily fills Alexandra with joy and tames her brother Nikos, but cannot convince his wife to return with him to Egypt.

The father rejects Alexandra's pleas to take her back with him. Instead, he tells her to stay and care for her mother and notify him if her condition worsens in even the tiniest way. There ensues nonetheless a period of contentment as Nikos remains reformed, and the family thrives on regular support payments from the father. All this changes, however, when Nitsa receives what she has been awaiting: a letter from Sotiris, informing her that he is in Geneva. Even though the letter does not invite her to join him, Nitsa experiences a miraculous recovery, practically leaps from her bed, and sets about moving the entire family to Geneva, ending the first part of the novel.

Sotiris has left Geneva for Paris a few days before the family arrives. They send word of their arrival and again wait to hear from him. After they have pawned everything they own, Alexandra supports them all by playing piano in a theater. The mother is now bedridden for good, utterly exhausted by her longing for Sotiris.

The family lives in a *pension* that mirrors the structure of the external world as well as the edifice of Alexandra's inner world. The lives of its inhabitants, all foreigners in Switzerland and all people who have somehow "strayed from the straight path" (in the terms of the novel's Greek title), reflect and affect those of the main characters. A catastrophic denouement is objectified in the gradual decay, decline, and eventual collapse of the *pension*, like the fall of houses in ancient Greek literature.

Nikos meets Emma, a Swiss girl who is convinced he is rich and tries to force him to marry her by giving birth to his child. Alexandra meets Kostas, an educated but narrow-minded and self-satisfied Greek whom she idolizes and adores with the same blind, self-denying monomania with which her mother adores Sotiris, but without her mother's physical passion. Shrouded by the deadening gloom of Geneva weather, the constant nagging of economic hardship, and a painful sense of separation from Greece, the characters make their way along their crooked paths.

Another "romance" is played out between Mimi, the *pension* owner's daughter, and Gregoreas, a wealthy Greek staying at the *pension* who "pulled her from the straight path." The rapid collapse of the entire house begins when Mimi is predictably abandoned by her "phony-fiance" and nearly dies of a self-induced abortion. Soon after, Alexandra's mother suffers a stroke after receiving a long-awaited letter from Paris telling her that Sotiris is sick and in prison. She lives only long enough to see Sotiris one last time from her hospital window, as he is rushing to see her upon his release, driven by a telepathic dream such as motivate many characters in Nakos's works.

Among other residents of the *pension* are Adamian, a sophisticated young Armenian woman who becomes Alexandra's friend; a lascivious Polish man; and a tubercular Greek schoolteacher and classical scholar who dies in Alexandra's arms. After a very few hopeful events, mingled always with foreboding omens, a rapid succession of disastrous events is initiated when an icon falls off a wall in the *pension*. An innocent orphan, Rosa, is raped by the Pole; Alexandra's surrogate "mother," the *pension* owner, dies; her good friend Sasha, a militant Communist, leaves for Russia; her lover, Kostas, becomes gravely ill, and Alexandra literally moves into the clinic to nurse him; her brother Nikos commits suicide; Mimi's new fiance is murdered on the eve of their wedding.

When Alexandra's beloved Kostas is released from the hospital, he goes off to the mountains with his sister, who gives Alexandra a box of chocolates in thanks for her service to Kostas. Jobless, homeless, and penniless, Alexandra has given up everything for Kostas. When she receives a letter informing her that he has returned to Greece to marry a rich woman, she determines to kill herself, but at the last moment she is presented with a purpose in life: her brother Nikos's lover, Emma, about to marry a young man from her village, gives Alexandra her baby by Nikos.

Alexandra: Observer and Victim

Alexandra is an arch-innocent of mythic proportions—as one critic puts it, "the Holy Virgin in Hell."[4] When Nikos is warned that his sister is being exposed to a corrupt environment in the *pension,* he is unperturbed: "The filth will pass over her without touching her" (212).[5] Alexandra's innocence makes possible her objective account of the lives of the people around her, so their strengths and weaknesses emerge without direct comments from her. For example, one of the most sympathetic characters, the Armenian woman Adamian, is clearly a prostitute, but Alexandra seems to have no idea or at least no opinion about her friend's profession.

While she faithfully describes the people and events around her, Alexandra claims not to understand them. When her friend Sasha tells her that he and his friends are returning to Russia to take part in the revolution, she says, "I didn't exactly know which revolution he was talking about" (345), even though she had been playing "The Internationale" at their meetings as a favor to Sasha.[6] Even after he spends a night explaining communism to her, Alexandra says, "Of course I didn't understand everything Sasha told me... But what did it matter? The sense didn't escape me any more..." (349). The approach, which is reminiscent of Katina's reaction to her half-brother George's communist theories in *The Deflowered One,* sidesteps the specifics of political dogma.

Finally, Alexandra's innocence makes her a perfect foil to expose the absurdity of current social values by following them to their logical conclusions. For example, Kostas tells her that he cannot think of having sex with her because she is a virgin, so she logically determines to alter her condition in order to please him. When he is furious rather than pleased, Alexandra is genuinely shocked. Her literal interpretation of Kostas's double standard throws into relief the senselessness of his value system.

Alexandra's night job as a piano accompanist at the Carouge Theater symbolizes her place in the novel's world. She is the exploited, ignored accompanist, wasting her considerable talents in support of others. Her apt description of a conceited tenor's attitude toward her is typical:

He doesn't look at me, nor does he greet me... He is totally ignorant of my existence and my presence... And even though I accompany him on the piano every night, . . . what has he got to do with me, a drop of a person? For him I am like the piano stool... (197)

This passage is part of the section of the book that represents Alexandra's psychological nadir, in which she is portrayed playing piano at the theater, sick, exhausted, her back and fingers shot through with pain. The entire section is written in the present tense; Nakos repeatedly employs a switch to the present at moments of emotional intensity; for example, when Alexandra goes to bed with Kostas for the first time (319), and when she receives his letter informing her that he is getting married (395). Alexandra's wretched state in the theater passage is also re-created by numerous pauses between short phrases, and by insistent repetition of the laments, "I'm tired," "I'm cold," "I cough."

Throughout the novel Alexandra is overlooked, slighted, and taken for granted. Her nineteenth birthday passes, totally forgotten by everyone. The novel's happy ending, moreover, consists not of her gaining recognition, but of her determining to serve yet another creature: Nikos's child.

Nikos: The Other Side

Destitute, depressed, and hounded by the shrewish woman he lives with, Nikos commits suicide. Alexandra says, "losing him, it was as if I had lost half of my own self" (356). Nikos can indeed be seen as the other half of Alexandra.[7] She is the good child; he is the bad. She allows none of her resentment nor anger to surface; he shows none of his tenderness nor love. Throughout the novel Nikos's development parallels Alexandra's. When she becomes aware of sex, he becomes aware of Despina, the maid. Nikos acts out her impulses: he sets fire to the family's house in Athens just when Alexandra feels the fires of sexual awakening, when she repeatedly refers to herself as "burning up."[8]

Nikos and Alexandra share the same feelings toward their (her) father and their mother, toward Sotiris, and toward leaving Athens. When Alexandra meets Kostas, Nikos meets Emma. While Alexandra constantly bemoans Nikos's waste of his artistic talent drawing sketches for tourists, she wastes her own talent by accompanying buffoons at the theater. The narrative often follows Nikos in actions and thoughts, when it is ostensibly Alexandra's first-person narrative. These two parts of Alexandra's character are seeking synthesis when Alexandra becomes attached to Sister Pagratia, a masculine woman, and Nikos begins spending time with Pagratia's brother, a feminine man. Nikos dies when Alexandra is with Kostas in the clinic, having forsaken everything—literally, half her self—for Kostas. Finally, in the end, Nikos's child becomes hers.

Alexandra sets out to commit suicide but does not do so. If Nikos represents the negative side of her, then his suicide corresponds to the death of one side of her. If that is the case, his is the hopeless, desperate side, the side that is the offspring of Nitsa's fatal love for Sotiris. Since Alexandra does not live out this fate with Kostas, happily that side of her dies. Nikos was the part of her that willingly preferred death to life, the crippled self, as Nikos himself was lame. His death then is part of the positive ending for Alexandra, representing her freedom from these qualities of her own character.

Coming of Age without Sex

The Lost is an account of Alexandra's coming of age, and this includes her introducton to sex. In fact, she searches endlessly for love without coming to terms with sex at all, and her encounters with sexuality are all traumatic. She never integrates sex into her life.

As a schoolgirl in Athens, Alexandra first experiences love in the form of a crush on an older girl whom she adores from afar. One day her mother discovers a lock of Violetta's lovely blond hair, which Alexandra managed to buy from another student at great cost. Convinced that her daughter is having a sexual relationship with the older girl, her mother beats her mercilessly. Alexandra is unable to imagine what she has done wrong, for she is quite innocent of sex. In fact, it is her mother who is obsessed with it.

Alexandra is exposed to sex through her brother Nikos. When she begs to be left alone, saying she is "unwell," he leers at her knowingly. Nikos is the child of the intense and destructive passion between Nitsa and her cousin Sotiris. He himself makes a display of his interest in Despina, the maid, and his younger sister is his unwilling witness:

> My brother had a strange scorn for every woman. . . . However, he liked to look at women... I had caught him many times with his eyes fixed on Despina's fat legs and looking steadily at her breasts. His lips got dry then and he wet them with his tongue. Despina also liked Nikos's desire for her. I often heard them bantering in the kitchen. It disgusted me. (101)

Although Alexandra is aware of Nikos's sexual games, she does not understand them. When she hears that Despina is going out at night to "do a favor" for the milkman, she has no idea what the nature of that favor might be.

Alexandra's adolescence, her taking residence in a new, sexual self, is reflected metaphorically in her move, with her family, to a new house near Lycabettos Hill, following the destruction by fire of the house in the old section of Plaka. Spring has arrived; Alexandra is fifteen and restless. Her budding sexuality is borne in upon her symbolically during the dizzyingly hot noon hour when most people are asleep and spirits are believed to roam. Feeling an unaccountable urge to weed the garden, Alexandra comes upon an ancient tomb which brings her face to face with her heritage as a woman and as a Greek. She stares at the tomb:

I saw a beautiful woman's body, with her breasts high and perfectly round. Sitting on her lap was a large Satyr... From the middle down, however, things were strangely mixed up... The Satyr's thighs covered her legs... The Satyr had a human head with a little pointed beard. His eyes sparkled with mischief. What was that air with which he was looking at the woman? He was pressing his body against hers with such pleasure!... It made you tremble... (104)

Stunned by this apocalypse, Alexandra stumbles into the house to get some water, only to come upon Nikos and Despina enacting a similar scene:

But as I passed through the second yard, in front of Despina's room, I heard something like sighs, as if people were whispering... I stopped involuntarily, and turned to see what was happening. And through the half-open door, I saw the maid lying on her back, but she had her head turned toward the wall... From her open blouse, her whole chest was showing, big and white, with the nipples deep red, I remember... Nikos was sitting next to her with his back to me. He was asking her for something in a choked, unrecognizable voice. He had one hand on her thigh, and he was slowly moving it up. Despina stretched her body, struggled, as if she liked it but yet did not want it... All of a sudden she yelled at Nikos in a stifled voice: "Not there! Higher, dummy!" And then she writhed and moved like a woman possessed. (104)

Like the heroines of Nakos's early stories, Alexandra reacts to sex with overwhelming revulsion: "How I despised both of them!"

Alexandra's first experience with a man occurs when she fights off the Pole's advances at the *pension* in Geneva. The older man has expressed interest in her piano playing and has introduced her to an eminent piano teacher. However, he expects recompense for his kindness, and as soon as he catches the young woman alone, he pounces:

His heavy, panting breath stroked my face... He was all red and distorted... His mouth searched for mine... Oh, no! No! I didn't want it at all... I pulled away from him violently... I was so frightened, I just barely kept from screaming. I detested him. I had never been kissed!... And I kept pulling back and pushing him away. (183)

The man begins to curse Alexandra for being ungrateful, and she is confused by his attack. He takes advantage of her confusion to press his mouth against hers. When she closes her eyes so as not to have to look at his face, he calls her "a little hedonist," and he interprets her lack of composure as lust: "Look, how pale you got, and how your hands froze. Ah! You little Eastern women, what hot creatures you are!" (183).

Alexandra is the object of a similar attack one night on her way home from the casino. She is saved that time by Señora Lola, a huge motherly singer who remarks, "Men! . . . They have nothing on their minds except their things..." (200).

Despite her adoration of Kostas, Alexandra never thinks of having sex with him, until she learns that he is having an affair with a married woman. When she confronts him, Kostas tells her that he needs a mistress because he cannot make love to Alexandra, since she is a virgin. Alexandra goes to a doctor and disposes of her virginity "scientifically," then waits for the right moment to "surprise" Kostas. (This is reminiscent of Nakos's "The Story of the Virginity of Miss Tade," in which the heroine is about to give up her virginity to a doctor, for the sake of the man she loves.) That moment comes when they are stranded overnight in an isolated country inn. Poor Alexandra is shocked to see that her loss of virginity doesn't please Kostas any more than her possession of it did. Quite the contrary, he bolts from the bed, cursing her: "How can I ever trust you again?" he screams. "How do I know you didn't go down with all the men at the casino?" (322). Just as with the Pole, and with her mother when she was a girl adoring Violetta from afar, the angelically innocent Alexandra is accused of sexual excesses.

Alexandra never makes an explicit judgment about sexuality, but her associations with sexual activity are always negative, and she never integrates an understanding of sexuality with her need for love. For example, she cannot understand why her father does not accept her in place of a wife. Her belated attempt to establish a physical relationship with Kostas only drives him further away. In the end, happiness comes in the form of love not for a man but for a child.

An Awakening to Social Consciousness

The Lost is a personal account of its heroine's coming into adulthood, spanning roughly the ages seven to twenty-one. At the same time, however, it is a tableau portraying with moving verisimilitude the injustice of an economic and social system that contributes to people's suffering. It has been seen, for example, that much of Alexandra's personal suffering, and that of other women in the novel, is a direct result of their victimization as women.

Alexandra's awakening to an awareness of sexuality coincides with her introducton to social injustice and poverty. At about the time that she enters adolescence, her mother's cousin Sotiris notices her. One day he takes her with him on a combination business trip/outing. First, they visit a business associate, a rich man who is practically paralyzed by his own fat. All together, they visit the man's mines where he talks to the workers while his fancily dressed sister-in-law complains that he's too lenient with them. While the men attend to business, Alexandra is sent to wait with a worker's family, ostensibly headed by Lenio, a girl of perhaps twelve who has had to leave school in order to care for the newborn baby so that her mother can continue to work. Lenio toils, philosophizes, and laments like an old woman, while her brothers act out a fatal mine accident for a game. For the first time, Alexandra sees a child working like a slave: a theme that recurs throughout Nakos's journalism as well as her fiction and reappears in *The Lost* in the character of the orphan child Rosa, who works in the laundry opposite the *pension* in Geneva. Thus Alexandra's social and sexual awakening coincide.

It has already been noted that the *pension* in Geneva is a microcosm of the larger world. The theater where Alexandra plays piano is yet another microcosm; it is an underworld inhabited by a bevy of grotesques. The audience is like "a many-headed monster, shouting"; the women at intermission look like "little monkeys, as they hold up their little mirrors." The performers too constitute a bestiary: the tenor "struts like a peacock"; the young singers "meow like newborn kittens" (198). The toppling queen of this underworld is Señora Lola, the good-hearted aging singer who is thrown out to make way for the young in accordance with the laws of society. But even Lola is grotesque: "The sweat runs down her forehead and furrows her face which is plastered with powder" (197). The young singer who is replacing her, however, is far worse: "Pepita sings off-key in a cold voice, passing out insipid smiles... How can this be compared to poor Lola's warm voice. But she is nineteen years old... 'Bravo!... Bravissimo!...' her countrymen shout, and they shower her with flowers" (198). Their vapid values lead the audience to prefer Pepita simply because she is younger. Señora Lola is the only person in the theater who cares about Alexandra, and she is cast out.[9]

The theater is only a small reflection of the general injustice that characterizes the world of *The Lost* and the relationships between the people who inhabit that world.

Men against Women

The world of *The Lost* is unjust generally, but it is particularly unfair to women. The novel is filled with images of women who are fooled, taken advantage of, led astray by men. The prototypical male/female encounter is the love relationship, and in this novel, as in all of Nakos's early work, it is one that ends badly for everyone, most particularly for women.

When Alexandra is a young child living with her godmother, the young woman who takes care of her, Asimina, falls in love with a Serb who promises to marry her. Following his instructions, she goes to town and buys her trousseau from the Serb's friend. Then she waits all day in vain for her fiance. Walking back with Alexandra at night, Asimina crumples in the road, sobbing. She later learns that the Serb had arranged the ruse with the storekeeper in order to rob her of her dowry. "That was the end of Asimina's love," Alexandra comments as she recounts the story. "And it was the first love story I heard" (25).

The Holy Virgin in Hell: The Lost

This first love story is portentous. When Kostas abandons Alexandra years later, and she is wandering the streets of Geneva in despair, she recalls this image:

> I don't know why, just like that, I suddenly remember a wide road, and a woman, seated next to a ditch, crying... Soon this woman takes shape. It's Asimina, who is crying for her lost love. I am a child beside her, watching her... (398)

The love affair between Mimi, the *pension* owner's daughter, and the Greek Gregoreas follows the same pattern, as did Mimi's mother's story before her. Nowhere in *The Lost* do a man and a woman live happily ever after.

Although both women and men suffer as a result of love relationships, there is a crucial difference in their experiences. The men exercise their own wills, rejecting the love of women who truly love them, either because they love less worthy women (for example, Alexandra's father loves Nitsa, who does not love him, rather than the godmother who does), or because they prefer to marry for money (for example, Gregoreas and Kostas). The women, on the other hand, suffer because the men they love reject them.

There are, of course, women who operate within the corrupt system to exploit men. Such a one is Emma, Nikos's Swiss lover, but her efforts are a mockery since the "rich Greek" she is bent on snaring is really destitute. Adamian, the Armenian woman who is reminiscent of the Jewish mistress Vartoui in *The Deflowered One,* goes with men for their money, but she herself realizes, "When I hit forty, then it's a different tune..." She explains that she had no other choice: "There in the Caucasus my parents were rich. They managed to raise me to do nothing. To be a 'lady' " (285). In other words, Adamian has no other means of support, so she is herself a victim.

Strikingly, all the women in this novel are alone. Some are courageous: Sister Pagratia, who comes to help Alexandra's family after Sotiris has fled Athens and everyone else has turned against them; Louiza, Alexandra's adored French teacher; and Mme Dubois, the *pension* owner whose words encourage Alexandra: "The loneliness I felt in my life gave me pride, and this was my strength" (343). Others are defeated by their loneliness: Alexandra's mother; Mimi Dubois as she appears at the end; and Alexandra's beloved godmother, who moves to Paris after the child Alexandra is taken away from her, where she is reported to have died in misery.

A vast gulf separates men and women. Accused by Kostas of running around with all the men in the theater, Alexandra realizes, "So no matter how much you open your heart to him, a man never understands you..." (324). Kostas in his turn complains, with equal justification, "You girls don't understand... That's our ordeal... You see the man you love through all the romanticism that fills your brains..." (297). Again and again the men rail, "You women . . . ," and the women counter, "You men. . . ." Alexandra likes a defrocked Greek priest named Kyrillos because "He wasn't like other men. He didn't have that abrupt manner. You weren't afraid of him" (248). But Kyrillos is a poor model, for he is impotent.

As if by way of breaking this stalemate between men and women, two of the most favorably portrayed characters in the novel are androgynous: Sister Pagratia, the nun whom Alexandra admires and loves, has a "masculine voice" and an awe-inspiring manner.[10] Her kind brother, to whom Nikos forms an attachment, loves housekeeping, cooking, and crocheting lace. In this way Nakos seems to suggest that both men and women are the victims of their stereotyped roles. But both Pagratia and her brother live outside society: she in a convent, and he in a mental asylum. It is not shown how their androgynous qualities could be integrated in a life within the society where Nikos tells his sister that she is stupid and then adds, to comfort her, "But it's not your fault; you're a woman" (101).

Love as a Scourge

In a scheme where men and women understand each other so little, it is not surprising that love makes no one happy. Nitsa's love for Sotiris causes her family's lifelong misery and creates, as Alexandra says, "that suffocating atmosphere that I breathed since

I was little in the house in Athens" (255), the atmosphere that pervades the novel as well. Everyone has the knack of choosing impossible or inappropriate partners in love.

What is love, as portrayed in *The Lost?* For certainly love is what the novel is about. Alexandra repeatedly refers to her mother's love for Sotiris as "a sickness," a "curse for both of them" (133). Her own love for Kostas is much the same, although she herself does not have the same clarity in identifying it as such. "This isn't called love any more," her friend Adamian tells her. "It's a scourge" (390). Alexandra is humiliated by her love, and she knows it: "I sat in a corner and looked at him, like a dog watching its master" (252). Later, when Kostas tells her to stop coming around:

> I didn't speak... I just smiled fearfully... "Oh, Kostas, Kostas," I said to myself, "if you had any idea how much I love you..." Surely I must have the soul of a dog... Otherwise there's no explanation... Yes, no matter how much you scorn it and beat it, it keeps coming back and looks into your eyes... (326)

Alexandra realizes, "What an annoying thing that is for others," but she is helpless to act otherwise. This is the same scathing view of love, coupled with the same ironic self-caricature, that is the focus of the stories Nakos wrote at this time, "Love," and "Spring Invitation."

Alexandra gives herself up to Kostas: "He guided, as it were, my thought and my reading" (236), so she feels like less rather than more of a person because of him: "Never had I felt myself so much of a nothing" (222). Since she feels like nothing, that's how she acts: "Yes, he reads and I look at him. . . . I sit in a corner of his room and imagine that I am kissing his feet and kneeling before him, or that I become a rug so he can walk on me. . . . When I see Kostas I get paralyzed and I can't utter a word..." (288). And so it is not surprising when, after Kostas leaves her, she says, "It was as if I had lost my own self" (393) because indeed she had given her own self over to him.

Alexandra suffers deeply when Kostas leaves her. She would do anything to have him back. And yet, if her behavior until then is an indication of what her life with him would have been, she is fortunate that he left. When he becomes ill, she abandons everything in her life and moves into the clinic with him. Looking forward to her life with Kostas, Alexandra thinks:

> I'll never ask him for anything. I'll never be a burden to him either. Just so he lets me sit in a corner, take care of him and look at him. If he wanted us to live together, I would cook for him, I would copy his manuscripts for him, I would take care of everything. . . . Just so I find some job, so I wouldn't be a burden to him. (366)

Just as the death of her son Petros could be seen as Katina's resurrection in *The Deflowered One,* so Kostas's abandonment of Alexandra is her salvation from the fate she herself describes, and from her mother's fate: being destroyed by the "sickness" called "love."

The Hope and Despair of Parental Love

If it is hopeless for a woman to base her life on a man's love, what remains for her? Nakos's answer, according to *The Lost,* is a child's love. Alexandra's godmother was happy when the little girl was with her, and Adamian is happy and morally reformed at the end of the novel after she adopts the orphan, Rosa. Indications are that Alexandra will be happy with her brother Nikos's child. There seems, strangely, not to be enough room for both lover and child in this gloomy world.

Nitsa's passion for Sotiris left none for her children. Neither did the father think of Alexandra's welfare when he left for Egypt in the first place, nor when, after his visit, he refused to take his daughter back with him but rather asked her to stay and take care of the mother who had neglected her all her life. Alexandra sees this: "I went cold inside. He didn't think of me at all, and I loved him so much" (151). When Nikos and Alexandra throw themselves into his arms, he hardly notices them. Both parents use their children as pawns in their own games of love. Nitsa refuses to go to Egypt on the pretext that the climate wouldn't be good for the children, but when she wants to go to damp, dark Geneva to follow her lover, she pretends that it is for their education. Thus rejected by both parents, Alexandra searches for and temporarily finds substitutes for parental love. Her attachment to Kostas represents her attempt to replace her father. She also finds a series of women who take the place of her mother.

Alexandra's first mother-substitute is her godmother. Seeing her with her father, the child thinks, "It would be so lovely if the three of us could live here" (18). In Geneva the *pension* owner, Mme Dubois, takes the place of Alexandra's mother who is by then totally distracted by her pining for Sotiris. Mme Dubois in turn looks to Alexandra as a replacement for her own daughter who has turned to the streets following her disappointment in love for Gregoreas. "How I love your eyes, my child. They're serene and pure..." Mme Dubois tells Alexandra. "I wish my daughter still had such eyes" (174). When the *pension* owner dies, it seems to Alexandra "that I was losing my mother for the second time." A third mother figure is the older singer at the Theater Carouge, Señora Lola, who watches out for the young pianist and worries over her health.

Although as a child Alexandra is full of resentment toward her mother, when she grows up, she loves her despite her weaknesses, and Nitsa does finally come to appreciate her daughter, if only a little. But from the time they move to the new house near Lycabettos Hill, it is the daughter who takes care of the mother rather than the other way around.

Alexandra adores her father in the best Freudian tradition. She is jealous of her beautiful mother:

I could never understand why Mother had such success... Me, for example, who had a pretty face according to Nikos, no one ever looked at me. Maybe it was because I was skinny and short. (163)

Alexandra is constantly hurt because her father is indifferent to her and thinks only of his wife. Yet she continues to behave toward him as if she could take her mother's place. One time, when he is gazing at his wife Nitsa who doesn't notice him at all, Alexandra "bent and embraced him." She invites him to take a walk in the park: "Come, let's go out to Dexameni . . . before we go to sleep..." (149). When she thinks she will return with him to Egypt, she exults:

> How lovely it would be to live, the two of us alone... We would rent a small house. Of course it would have to have a small garden with a magnolia tree... And I would do the housework... I even thought about how we would arrange it. The dining room would be there. After that the office. In the evening, I would wait for Father to return from work, I would have the table set with a vase of flowers in the middle... Then we would read. (151)

This is more a romantic than a filial fantasy. Alexandra has seen her mother putting flowers on the table for Sotiris. For Alexandra, moreover, reading with a man constitutes the deepest intimacy. This is explicit in another of her fantasies. When she hears that a young Deputy was infatuated with her mother Nitsa, Alexandra dreams of having an admirer of her own:

> I dreamt I was tall and beautiful like Mother. Everyone was looking at me. "What would you like to do best of all tonight?" asked my Deputy who was also young and handsome. And I answered: "To read together..." (58)

It may not be insignificant that the Egyptian city in which the father lives is named Alexandria.
 Alexandra never overcomes her bitterness over her father's rejection of her and never understands why she could not take the role of his wife. When she learns that he has remarried in Egypt, she is unforgiving. "But he wouldn't take me with him to keep house, to keep him company, and read together. Well let him stay with his 'logical and calm young woman,' since he preferred a stranger to me..." (253). At the end, after Kostas has gone off and she is left with nowhere to go, Alexandra again thinks of her father with the bitterness of a spurned lover:

> But why did he have to get married?... It was still a grief to me, even if I had hid it from myself. Yes, since then I had gone cold, and

The Holy Virgin in Hell: The Lost

something broke inside me... I didn't answer his letters, and whatever he sent as a gift I sent back. (364)

Since *The Lost* is Alexandra's vision, it seems likely that there is a connection between the impossibility of replacing her mother in her father's affections and the impossibility of achieving happiness with any man.

Isolation and Loneliness

The world of *The Lost* is a world of injustice, emotional and physical deprivation, and overwhelming loneliness. Each person is isolated. Connections between individuals are temporary at best, more often superficial or spurious. This theme is reiterated as clearly as it is demonstrated. Alexandra says of her mother and Sotiris, "Their life seemed to me like a bad dream, frightening and sad. An uninterrupted struggle for each one to escape loneliness, without ever succeeding" (66). One cannot hope to escape isolation, but merely to forget it for a time.

Sotiris himself is not a villain but another victim of isolation. During the period when he befriends Alexandra, he tells her about his life as a restless young man and talks of the need "to have a person in the world, a true friend, to open your heart to, to forget your isolation" (105). He too has suffered from the hopelessness of his love for Nitsa. When Alexandra asks him what work he did as a young man in Europe,

My uncle laughed. "My work? At that time my most important work was to find a place to rest the love that was torturing me... Do you think that was easy? Just when you think you've buried your love in a certain city, one fine night the memory is waiting for you, all alive, as soon as you find yourself alone, and so you wander as if in Hell without peace anywhere. (107)

When Alexandra meets Kostas she finds a temporary reprieve from this human condition: "His memory accompanied me everywhere. I didn't feel loneliness inside me any more" (224). But by the end of the novel she has realized, painfully, that the reprieve was temporary. As she says when her friend Sasha announces that he is about to leave for Russia, "It seems to be my fate that whoever I love leaves me" (346).

It has been seen that Nakos favors a structure in her fiction that brings her protagonist to a spiritual low point twice in the work: once at the middle and once just before the end. In *The Lost* the first low ebb is dramatized in the description of the Carouge Theater as a kind of underworld in which Alexandra suffers, forgotten. The second low point, just before the end, contains the novel's main pessimistic image, its central dark vision. That is Alexandra's confrontation of her total isolation.

This isolation is borne in upon her when Kostas leaves for the mountains with his sister, after Alexandra has given up everything to devote herself entirely to caring for him in his illness. As soon as the train carries him away, her narrative slips into the present tense: "I turn toward the town alone" (363). One by one, Alexandra recalls and searches in vain for the people and places she knew before she forsook everything to nurse Kostas. The only loved one she finds is a picture of Christ in a bookstore window. The resemblance between Christ and herself is clear: "My God, what a sad head Christ has... Everyone has left him... He is alone..." (367). Again the short phrases and repeated pauses function to re-create her sense of desolation and despair.

This realization drives Alexandra nearly to suicide, as she walks alone at night:

A woman walks out on a terrace and leans against the railing. She looks at the darkness in the garden. I'm so close to her, yet so far away! "What loneliness, what loneliness!" I think. "Each one of us lives and dies alone, with our pain." And a wave of despair takes hold of me. (399)

This bleak vision dominates *The Lost,* which was written when Nakos was bitterly depressed. Her father had just died, and her lover Ventiris had abandoned her, after she had moved back to Greece to be with him. Furthermore, she was living with her mother in a country she had left as a child, where she had few friends (she found Greek women of her class frivolous and superficial).[11] Finally, she was grievously overworked at three jobs and, for the first time, was exposed to the virulent anti-feminine sentiments of Greek male colleagues.

Nonetheless, as was seen in the discussion in Chapter One, Nakos deplores nihilism and believes strongly that literature should give hope to its readers. Moreover, the act of writing was for her a way of reaffirming her own hope. She finds such hope in a philosophy of love for others as well as religious faith which is represented in the section quoted in which Alexandra found "a friend" in the picture of Christ. The structure outlined contributes to this vision as well, for the despair Alexandra experiences is relieved by a sudden upsurge of events and spirits.

After Kostas has left Geneva, Alexandra is rescued from the limbo of literally wandering the streets by her old friend Adamian, the Armenian woman from the *pension*. Adamian's adopted daughter, Rosa, comes upon Alexandra in a park. Adamian takes Alexandra into her home. This alone, however, does not give Alexandra a purpose in life. Her purpose comes, just when she is about to deliver a suicide note to Adamian, in the form of a child of her own, the baby which had been born to Emma, fathered by Nikos. Thus the novel ends on a note of hope rather than despair.

One critic summarizes the impact of *The Lost* as "the tragedy of a person: the autobiographical heroine; the tragedy of a family; the tragedy of Greeks abroad; finally, the most universal tragedy of human loneliness and especially of woman's loneliness."[12] All this it is indeed. And it is also a social document, for Nakos demonstrates that these tragedies are intertwined with and caused by the social and economic systems of the times.

Chapter Five
"Never Love a Man": *Nafsika*

After World War II and its attendant horrors, as depicted in the stories of *The Children's Hell,* and following her mother's death, Lilika Nakos settled in Europe once again, and once again she wrote in French rather than Greek. While she was writing for French and Swiss magazines and newspapers, she wrote the novel *Mrs. Doremi* and a short novella called *Nafsika* which she rewrote in Greek and had published upon her return to Greece in 1953. Nakos has commented that she has particular affection for this little book. Her affection is easy to share; the novella is lyrical and moving, suffused with poetry and mysticism.

Although it was written later than *Boetian Earth* and *Mrs. Doremi, Nafsika* was published before those works. Moreover, because of similarities in themes and tone, *Nafsika* can be seen as the third work, forming a tripartite unit with Nakos's first two major works: *The Deflowered One* and *The Lost.* It resembles these and other early works in a number of ways. It is a first-person narrative, told by a lonely and troubled child who feels alienated from her parents. Based on Nakos's first experience with expatriation when her mother took her to live in Marseilles at the age of six, the story opens on a Greek island but soon moves to Marseilles where most of the action takes place.

Nakos has commented that the character of the mother in *Nafsika* resembles her own mother: a frail and warmhearted intellectual. In contrast, the mothers in her other works are portrayed as frivolous and callous. Nakos returned to Switzerland after the German Occupation at least partly because her mother had just died in Greece. It may well be that *Nafsika* is, in some sense, a eulogy to her mother, who is re-created in this little book as a tragic and lovely heroine, idealized through her recasting as an island villager rather than the upper-class Athenian she was. In the earlier works, *The Deflowered One, The Lost,* and *Boetian Earth* as well as the short stories, the mother emerges as haughty and cold: superficial and narcissistic at best, cruel and rejecting at worst. In the later novel *Toward a New Life* the mother is sympathetic, but still coquettish and aristocratic, at least in her pretensions. *Nafsika* remains the single work in which the mother figure is idealized.

The portrait of the mother in this work contributes to the fact that this is Nakos's most feministic piece. It is especially impressive that she has managed to blend gracefully a potent social statement into a wistful and dreamlike narrative.

At times, the wind howling through *Nafsika* seems to whisper of *Wuthering Heights.* Like Emily Brontë, Lilika Nakos has seen visions. A believer in psychic phenomena, she recounts that when she was a young woman feeling particularly hopeless and dejected, she was staying at her family's home in the suburb of Ekali. As she lay in bed in her upstairs room, she saw Christ appear before her. She begged him to take her with him, but he said, "Not yet," and raised his arm to point outside: "Your place is with them." Shifting her gaze in the direction he indicated, she saw a grim tableau of gaunt, starving creatures. It was not until the German Occupation that she realized, when she saw those very faces again, that her vision had been prescient.

Nakos's belief in psychic phenomena has continued and deepened. She keeps beside her bed a copy of Yogananda's *Autobiography of a Yogi,* and she regrets the lack of availability of metaphysical literature in Greek. This mystical orientation has influenced all her writing to some extent; it is felt strongly in *Boetian Earth* and *Ikarian Dreamers.* Its influence is deepest, however, in *Nafsika.*

The Story

The novella opens on an unnamed island where the child-heroine Nafsika lives with her mother and grandmother and is cared for by a sensitive and dreamy young nursemaid named Marina. The mother, Lena, is devastated because her husband, a successful Athenian lawyer and politician, has left her to marry another woman. The grandmother decides to send Lena, with her little girl, to stay with an uncle in Marseilles to recover from her grief.

Far from finding relief, however, Lena and Nafsika become virtual prisoners in the shuttered house of the sinister uncle. Although they are not permitted to leave their attic room, a kindly Chinese servant named Fuji secretly allows the child to play in the yard, where she discovers that the uncle is keeping women imprisoned in his cellar. When the uncle is arrested for engaging in the white slave trade, Nafsika and her mother are freed. They go to live in Antibes (Côte d'Azur) on the estate of a benevolent Greek named Mr. Vrondzatos, whom Lena falls in love with and plans to marry.

While her mother returns to Marseilles to take care of the business of her uncle's property, Nafsika has a brief period of perfect happiness living in the country with a big French peasant named Mme Germaine. However, Lena soon takes the child back to the city, where a happy ending is forestalled by the mischievous intervention of a former maid in Vrondzatos's household who tells Lena the lie that Vrondzatos is the father of her child. Lena swoons, miscarries her own unborn baby, and dies. Nafsika's last chance for happiness is destroyed when her father takes her away from the kind Vrondzatos and packs her off to a boarding school in Switzerland.

The Structure

The opening section of *Nafsika* forms a Paradise Lost, a brief period of happiness for the child, close to her loving nursemaid and grandmother, close to nature, on an island. This is similar to the first section of *The Lost*, depicting Alexandra's brief childhood happiness with her godmother on her country estate.

Events proceed to a low ebb which occurs, as usual, precisely in the middle of the book and is reflected in Nafsika's collapsing physically when she hears a mesmerizing, wounding song and thus discovers that there are women imprisoned in her uncle's cellar. She is paralyzed, for the song affects her like a physical blow: "and I fell face down on the ground and began to cry. I was in pain as if a wound had opened inside me. That's how the old servant found me when he returned" (57).[1]

After this episode, events take a positive turn as police raid the house, arrest the uncle, and free Nafsika and her mother. Vrondzatos appears, and he and Lena fall in love. Nafsika likes her mother's friend, but she is particularly happy with Mme Germaine, a mother-substitute with whom she stays in the country. But after this brief upturn, events again plunge. Her mother takes her back to the evil-spirited house in Marseilles and soon dies of a miscarriage.

This series of mishaps leads to a second low point which occurs when a maid, Asimina, buries the aborted fetus in a special cemetery she has fashioned for unbaptized babies. As if bewitched by the song Asimina croons to the fetus, Nafsika lies down in the strange cemetery. Asimina pulls her up, as Fuji did in the earlier episode. Perceiving the significance of Nafsika's gesture, Asimina shrieks, "Get up, Nafsika, open your eyes. . . . You're not unbaptized and your place isn't here" (102). The child's attraction to death is like Alexandra's impulse to commit suicide at the end of *The Lost,* and a similarly mystical attraction to a peaceful death which draws the child in Nakos's short story "The Little Servant" to jump into a well. Nafsika, however, dies only symbolically. In fact, she recovers and returns to Marseilles and shortly thereafter is sent to Switzerland to suffer "alone in a foreign and unfriendly place" (107).

This novella is unlike both earlier and later novels but similar to many of Nakos's short stories in that its ending is sad. Nakos has not tacked on a hope-inspiring conclusion, as she has done in *The Deflowered One* and *The Lost* as well as most of the later works. The technique of ending with the heroine leaving for another place, however, is employed in the other books of this middle period, *Boetian Earth* and *Mrs. Doremi,* as well as *The Deflowered One.*

An Atmosphere of Magic and Myth

Nafsika is the only heroine Nakos has given an ancient rather than Christian name. In Homer's *Odyssey* Nafsika is King Alcinous's daughter, whom Odysseus finds playing with her handmaidens by the sea when he is washed up onto the shores of Phaeacia. An enchanting atmosphere of the sea, the mesmerizing rhythm of the tide, and the eery howling of the wind dominate *Nafsika* and give the entire work a haunting, mythic sense.

The windblown island where Nafsika spends the blissful first part of her life and of the book is like a dreamworld, in the way that the old nursemaid's paradisiacal home functions in *The Deflowered One*. Nafsika's nursemaid, furthermore, is a poetic and pained character whose very name is associated with the sea. Marina suffers from epilepsy, called *selinismo* (literally, "moonism"), as if she is particularly sensitive to the pull of the tides which dominate the island and indeed the whole atmosphere of the novella.

Marina is not the only woman with special sensitivity. The maid Asimina, in Marseilles, is like a white witch. Nafsika is a bit afraid of her because "as she herself said, she spoke with spirits and exorcised them" (87), and in fact Asimina predicts the evil that befalls the family.

The mother, too, with her delicate beauty, her long veil-like hair, and her eternal suffering, is like a strange spirit. The mother's power is dangerous to the child, even if it is not malicious. When Lena learns that her husband has divorced her, she clutches her daughter in a way that is frightening and suffocating to the child, who recalls:

She cried and cried, and her tears salted my mouth, and I was entangled in her hair as in a net. I was very frightened. Suddenly the window was opened by the wind which charged into the room and put out the candle. We remained embracing in the dark. My hands had frozen and I trembled all over, but not a word escaped my mouth. Then my grandmother ran to rescue me from my mother's embrace which was cutting off my breath. (21)

The anthropomorphic characterization of the wind emphasizes that it is a palpable and formidable force on the island. Marina says, "I love nothing but the wind... When I hear him fighting maniacially to uproot the island, when he raves and howls, ah, then I am happy" (13).

This haunting atmosphere is created as well by everpresent strains of music. The sound of the café-owner's flute fills the village's "deserted square with the palm tree which gave no shade" on the island. Both Marina and Nafsika sense the power of this melody:

It was always the same, monotonous and despairing, and it shook my childhood soul. It had the same effect on Marina, because she covered her ears and said loudly: "Damn the café owner and his flute... When I hear it, something inside me cracks and I'm afraid I'll have a seizure." (10–11)

Music is weird and enchanting, flowing from an unseen source, reminiscent of the sirens' song in *The Odyssey*.

Later, when Nafsika hears the singing of the imprisoned women in her uncle's house, it casts a veritable spell on her:

And suddenly a voice arose as if it wanted to sing to mourn something it had lost forever.

It was a long-drawn-out, monotonous, heartrending melody, which echoed strangely in this silent house with its closed shutters. And as this voice went on, it strengthened, filled the yard, the world, as if it wanted the grief it bore to reach the sky. Overcome by this melody, I couldn't move. (57)

Finally, when Nafsika lies down among the unbaptized ones, again she is overcome by a melody, as Asimina conducts the odd funeral:

And when she finished the grave, I saw her sit next to it and begin to sing slowly to it. It was a strange melody that sprang from inside her of its own will, like words which came from her heart. Softly, as she sang monotonously and mournfully, something like sleep suddenly came over me too... I felt like falling down right there on the earth, amid the daisies, and sleeping near the unbaptized ones. (102)

These magical strains weave through both sections of the novella: the happy fairyland of the island and the equally mysterious, jinxed Marseille.[2] A mysterious spirit is felt in another Nakos work, *Boetian Earth*, but there the fairy-tale quality is of a cheerful nature. *Nafsika* has a mournful air, a deep sense of grief and loss.

The Good and the Bad

Since *Nafsika* is a mythic world, its characters are clearly distinguished as good or bad, as are the characters of *The Deflowered One*. There are two types of women and two types of men. The good women love Nafsika; they are gentle, and they do not exploit men. On the contrary, they suffer because of men. They are, first of all, the mother Lena and the grandmother; then Marina, the island nursemaid; the peasant Mme Germaine; and the maid Asimina. As in *The Lost*, there are two types among these good women: the competent, independent ones who have learned to manage on their own, and those who have been broken by their mistreatment and loneliness.

Mme Germaine is a big, competent woman in the tradition of Sister Pagratia (*The Lost*) and a forerunner of Nakos's greatest heroine, Victoria (*Toward a New Life*). Mme Germaine is masculine: "She was tall and on her top lip she had a thick black fuzz like a moustache" (72). She is imposing: "No one got the better of her when she started to talk" (76). Nafsika is happy when she stays in the country with Mme Germaine who is affectionate and expansive and never loses courage nor complains. Even though her husband left her twice for younger women, she cheerfully took him back and now nurses him, since he is permanently paralyzed. Her robust spirit contrasts strikingly with Nafsika's mother's constant lament which has "poisoned" her daughter's soul.

Asimina is a maid who used to work for Vrondzatos and then went to work for Lena. She is a midwife and is powerful and wise. Like other Nakos midwives, she, ironically, has no children

"Never Love a Man": Nafsika   87

of her own. Asimina too was married to an unworthy husband, a smuggler. Now she is alone. Asimina is the most complex character in the book. She loves Nafsika and Lena, but the child is rather intimidated by her and does not adore her as she does Marina and Mme Germaine. Moreover, Asimina is the perpetrator of a strange and disturbing act: she shows Nafsika a bottle of alcohol containing her mother's aborted fetus.[3] Nafsika is traumatized by the sight, despite the fact that the maid's motives are apparently benign. Asimina chides, "At your age I was going with my mother and assisting at births, and you act like that? . . . Look, how she's trembling!... Oh, God, she's fainting..." Nakos turns her ironic edge on the child rather than the maid, who says, "You call these children today? They're not worth anything!" (96). Yet Asimina regrets the effect her revelation has on Nafsika. Furthermore, the moving, if macabre, funeral which Asimina gives the unborn fetus is an act of love:

She had wrapped it in a clean cloth and laid it in the earth as if in a little bed and carefully and lovingly she bent over it. She spoke to it, whispering something, perhaps words of love that it would never hear. (102)

Thus Asimina is a good, independent woman, trying to correct some of the injustice in the world.

A frailer sort of woman, more like Lena than Asimina, is Marina, the poetic, epileptic island girl whom Nafsika loves as a young child. A fisherman who wants to marry her is no match for the quick-minded and perceptive Marina. When she asks him, "Have you found any meaning in life?" the good-natured fellow is bewildered: "Meaning in life? What does that mean? I don't understand" (13). Marina's suffering resonates to Lena's despairing sobs and the howling of the wind.

Not all the women in *Nafsika* are good. As Asimina says, there are many women who "try to exploit others in order not to work" (105). The prototype of this sort of woman is Vrondzatos's villainous former maid who, according to the omniscient Asimina, lied about her child's paternity and "was a bad woman." Another bad woman is Vrondzatos's first wife who obstinately refuses to grant him a divorce. (In contrast, when Lena's husband divorces her, the implication is that justice would lie in Lena's preventing him from obtaining the divorce. The issue clearly is not divorce but the nature of the women involved.) Finally, Nafsika's father's second wife falls in line with the bad. She is hypocritical, cold, flirtatious, and superficial, like most upper-class characters Nakos portrays.

If Nafsika's mother is the prototypical good woman, her father is the prototypical bad man. He perpetrates injustice personally by rejecting Lena's love; economically, by using his wealth to manipulate; and politically, by being a member of Parliament. Lena is from an island; her husband is from Athens. She is of the people; he is of the upper class. The dichotomy could not be more clear-cut. When Nafsika visits her father in his office in Athens, he threatens: "Don't worry, you'll see what a father is worth when he has the money. If I want I'll make you two dance like French tops... with a horsewhip!" (25)

In the character of the uncle in Marseilles, money is again associated with evil. On one of the rare occasions when he visits Lena in her attic room, the uncle tells her: "There's only one God in the world: money" (60). Even as a child, Nafsika knows where the lines are drawn. "I don't like the rich," she announces to Marina, "because they're snobs" (17).

The bad characters are identified in numerous obvious ways. The father, for example, hates reading, while his wife has a passion for books. Similarly, he has no feeling for the country, open air, or nature, which are vital to both Nafsika and her mother.

Vrondzatos, the helpmate that falls in love with Lena, is the father's opposite, the prototype of a good man. He is faithfully selfless to the end. Although rich, he does not worship money nor use it to control people. Vrondzatos has another characteristic that identifies him as good: he plays the guitar, as Lena plays the piano. Music, like literature, is the domain of the good. But Vrondzatos is preyed upon by two evil women: his first wife and his former maid.

The dominant male and female characters are Nafsika's parents. Accordingly, there are more good women than good men. This is not to say, however, that there are no benevolent men in this novella. Besides Vrondzatos, the exploited Chinese servant Fuji and Marina's suitor Andreas are good characters as well. Like the women, they can be exploited and abused, but the women are the primary victims.

A Feminist View of Love and Marriage

Even though Andreas is a good man, Marina refuses to marry him because she trusts no man. She tells the child Nafsika,

"Man is woman's enemy. All her difficulties come from him. My father beat me to death and my brothers pulled my hair and tortured me. They all wanted my mother to be their slave in the house . . . . God help the woman who falls in the net of love for a man... No, I'll never get married." (12)

Similarly, Lena's last words to her daughter before she dies are: "Swear that when you grow up, you'll never love a man! I don't want you to be unhappy like me..." (92).

Love brings suffering (as it does in *The Lost* and *The Deflowered One*). At first Lena idolized her husband. As a result, she is later devastated:

As soon as my mother realized who the man she so adored really was, she literally nearly died. It seemed to her that the earth opened and swallowed her up, that nothing was stable and nothing mattered in the world any more. She shut herself up in her room, threw out even her books, and cried from morning until night in grandmother's house where she came and huddled like a wounded bird to its first nest. (19)

Lena longs to be independent. She refuses to accept Vrondzatos's offer that she be a guest in his villa, preferring to rent it from him. When her uncle says he will leave her his money, she assures him she wants no one's money; all she wants is a job, so she can earn her own. Furthermore, she wants her daughter "to study, to become independent, to work, so she won't need any man in order to live with dignity" (48). Lena epitomizes a victimized woman. She never has the opportunity to achieve the independence she craves.

A vision of women as exploited and mistreated is at the core of *Nafsika*. It is embodied most horrifically in the unseen women whom the uncle sells like merchandise. If Lena and Nafsika are virtual prisoners in the uncle's house (and, in a symbolic sense, in the world of men), the women in the cellar are literal prisoners locked behind barred windows. The scene in which Nafsika discovers the women is the turning point of the story. It represents her realization, not yet conscious, of the suffering of all the oppressed and of women in particular.

Personal Suffering in an Unjust World

Nafsika is the chronicle of the suffering of Lena and, as a result, of Nafsika. It is also a statement about social injustice, which is the external macrocosm corresponding to the personal injustice Lena suffers in love. The external world, in turn, is reflected in the characters' personal lives.

At the very start, Nafsika's nursemaid Marina gives her a sense of empathy with all those who are oppressed. Marina silently addresses the wind: "Howl, cry for those who suffer, for those who, without uttering a word, are treated unjustly" (13). This lament is a refrain which Nafsika later recalls.

The social and personal aspects of injustice are fused in the mother's divorce. After her collapse upon learning that her husband has divorced her and married another woman, Lena is seen by the village doctor, who exclaims, "But this is an injustice." The grandmother agrees:

"It's a great injustice, Doctor... Go try to find justice. He's a man, he's a lawyer, he's a wealthy member of Parliament; he has the power in his hands. What are we? Two poor women and we have no one to stand up for us in Athens. You need money for this kind of business with the courts. Where would we find it? Where shall a wretched woman ever find justice?" (22)

The Greek word "justice," *dikaio,* also means "right" in the sense of human rights. Women, like the poor, have no "rights" as a result of the lack of "justice." Just before the tragic denouement begins, a noisy demonstration by striking dockworkers is heard in the streets outside the uncle's house, where Lena now lives with Vrondzatos, who explains, "They are workers demanding their rights... The only people who have anything to fear are those who don't have clear consciences." Nafsika understands:

And then suddenly I remembered my friends the stokers on the French ship. I remembered how they lived amid the flames in the depths of the boat, while the day above them was laughing. . . . And suddenly I felt myself united with them, with all those who toil, for that was how my heart dictated. (80)

In the midst of this demonstration Fuji returns, exhausted and ill, to the house where he himself had been like a slave. Fuji takes the demonstration as a sign: "But now the time has come for Fuji to find what he longs for... Justice... Do you hear, my dear little lady, how many mouths are crying out for it?" (85). Ironically, Fuji is dying. Is it in death alone that one can find justice?

When he tells his story, Fuji counts women among the oppressed:

My parents sold me as a slave when I was little. When I was little, they beat me as if I had no soul. When I grew up, people cheated me, and when I grew old, they ate even my sweat... Oh, my little lady, now the oppressed of the earth are shouting, do you hear how they're shouting?... They're shouting for me and you. You're oppressed too... Wretched women are oppressed and bartered slaves... Oh, my dear little lady, I'm dying, but I tell you, I know [justice] will come one day... Open the door so she can come in, so I can see her face!... (85–86)

Since the dying Fuji refers to the feminine noun *dikaiosyni* ("justice") with the feminine pronoun, the effect is as though in his feverish delirium he expects justice to walk through the door in the form of a woman. The woman who comes through the door shortly thereafter, however, is not justice, but Vrondzatos's scheming former maid, hastening the undeserved tragedies of all the main characters. Although the desire for it is impassioned, the prospects for justice are grim.

Conclusion: The Greek Ideal

Nafsika is similar to Nakos's early work in its focus on a child's point of view, in its cynical portrayal of men and of love, in its European setting, and finally in the bleak vision it presents of personal tragedy and social injustice. However, the short work represents Nakos's development in a number of ways. The style, lyrical and smooth, is Nakos at her best and fully mature. Moreover, in keeping with the trend noted in Chapter One which Peter Bien has explained, the post-World War II infatuation with Greece that characterizes Greek fiction has taken root and is evident in this work as well. Whereas Alexandra in *The Lost* suffered as a child in Athens, and Katina in *The Deflowered One* finds only hardship and pain in her homeland, Nafsika's early experience on her home island is nothing less than idyllic, while the French city is dark and cruel.

The little book *Nafsika* is an important one in Nakos's canon. It combines a number of her accustomed themes in a particularly lovely and intense form, at the same time that it is her most feministic work and the one most palpably tinged with mysticism.

Chapter Six

Comic Lament on a Rocky Coast: *Mrs. Doremi*

As has already been recounted in Chapter One, Nakos left Greece following the ordeal of the German Occupation during World War II in which she had starved and been beaten and lost all those she loved, including her mother whom she had lived with and supported since her father's death in 1933. Having managed to leave Greece during the bitter Civil War, she arrived in Lausanne with nowhere to go and no money. In the midst of this despair, just as might happen in one of her novels, a friend appeared and told her that the editor of the Swiss magazine *Illustré* wanted her to write a story about Crete—a humorous story. Feeling anything but humorous, Nakos took an advance from the editor and wrote *En Crete,* which she later rewrote in Greek as *Mrs. Doremi,* recalling the nickname she had been dubbed by the students in Rethymnon, Crete, because she had taught them music.[1] Although Nakos's year in Crete (1933) had been a ghastly experience for her, she used it as the basis for her only comic novel.

The narrator and protagonist of *Mrs. Doremi* is again a young Greek woman who has lived abroad. Katerina Makri, born and raised in Paris, is living in Greece for the first time when the novel opens. She has been forced to seek work to support herself and her mother because her father has died. Unlike his counterpart in *The Deflowered One,* Katerina's father is characterized favorably through the recollections of those who knew him as generous, gregarious, and charming. His daughter dismisses his womanizing with good-hearted indulgence:

The only inheritance we found in his safe were about thirty photographs of half-naked women, ballerinas and singers who had sweetened the life of the deceased, as it appeared from their dedications. Truly, my poor father loved two things in his life: Paris and women. (8)[2]

This generous approach to her dead father sets the tone for the book, in contrast with the bitter gloom of earlier works.

Nor does Katerina resent her father for having left her poor: "This made me get to know life, to find out with what effort people get by here. Moreover, with this experience, the horizons of my life opened, and I got to know Greece, and to love her as she is with her good and bad" (8). Indeed, in keeping with the patriotic spirit engendered in World War II and seen also in *Nafsika,* this novel is an expression of love for Greece, represented in exaggerated proportions in the big, wild island halfway between Europe and Africa. *Mrs. Doremi* portrays an untamed Crete, where the high school students carry guns and knives, and an atavistic feud leads to bloody battle.

In *Mrs. Doremi* Nakos romanticizes Greece. As in *Boetian Earth,* rural villagers and their countryside are the true Crete which Katerina comes to love. The townspeople of Rethymnon are her enemies before they even meet her, and everything she does exacerbates their enmity, until she is forced to flee at the end. Yet this ending is not tragic.

The Story

Katerina arrives in Crete by stormy sea, full of fear of the future and longing for her native Paris. She is met on the boat by a "moustached colossus" fittingly named Heracles who plucks the tiny woman off her feet and drops her into the small launch that ferries them to shore. He takes her to the sorry-looking room which is the only one in town she may have, since everyone has heard dreadful things about her from a sinister character named Karderinakis who never ceases to spread malicious lies about her, for no reason other than his malevolent nature.

At school, Katerina is faced with enormous classes of 150 boys each. One day a veritable battle erupts in the classroom, the oldest boys firing pistols which they always carry, while the poor teacher crouches under the desk. On another occasion, a full-scale war breaks out in the town when a shepherd "kidnaps" a willing town girl who happens to be the high school principal's servant and the fianceé of Heracles, the huge man who met Katerina at the boat. The young men of the town take sides and fight it out, guns, casualties and all, as the townspeople gleefully watch the spectacle.

Katerina falls in love with a student, Lefteris, who is two years older than she. She befriends Sally, a British artist who lives in Lefteris' village. Sally is a liberated, spontaneous woman who outrages the narrow-minded townspeople but charms the sensible villagers as she does Heracles, who has fully recovered from the loss of his fianceé. The townspeople, meanwhile, continue to have it in for the poor young teacher, blaming her for such crimes as consorting with Sally, talking to a French Catholic priest, visiting a tubercular child, and corrupting Lefteris.

The anger of the Rethymnon society becomes venomous when the overworked teacher, given the additional load of teaching at the girls' high school, takes a group of girls on an excursion to a place she has discovered with a lovely view. She introduces the snickering students to the wretched "prisoners" who live there, none other than the local prostitutes. This blunder is Katerina's last. The principal advises her to go immediately to talk to the Superintendent in the capital town of Chania. The Superintendent informs Katerina that the town is out for her blood, and she leaves Crete for good on the next boat, bid goodbye by Sally, Heracles, and a last-minute clutch of her favorite village boys who have dragged, shoved, and coaxed a donkey on the bus from Rethymnon as a going-away present.

Katerina's untimely departure from Crete is nostalgic, but not tragic. In contrast with Alexandra's desperate fear of losing her job in *The Lost,* Katerina repeatedly expresses her indifference: if she is fired, so much the better. She will return to her beloved Paris. Her expulsion is more tragic for the students who have come to love her.

Familiar Structure in a Light Vein

The familiar pattern of peaks and plunges in events and in the emotional development of the protagonist can be seen in *Mrs. Doremi*, but the novel's light tone is reflected in the nature of the events and their impact.

Katerina's nadir, occurring in the middle of the book, is an emotional crisis, but the effect, for the reader, is comic. The young teacher mounts the podium at the high school to lecture on the life of a great musician to several hundred of the oldest boys. Terrified from the start, poor Katerina gets no further than the composer's name, Gluck, which sounds so funny to the boys that:

> they began to bellow all together, first softly, then louder, until they nearly brought the roof down with the roar... Gloo, Glooooooo! Gloooooooooooooooooook!... In other words, as they say in music, they began with the "Gloooo" crescendo until they reached fortissimo, so that the windows shook with the noise. Then they lowered their voices gradually, until they quieted and returned to pianissimo. (94)

Comic as the scene is in the retelling, Katerina flees the room, the school, the town, in despair: "The tears now flowed down my face unrestrained. I felt myself suddenly very isolated and sad in a strange place. . . . Oh if only I could go far away from here..." (95).

This emotional plunge, however, is immediately followed by an upswing as Lefteris seeks her out to apologize for his fellow students, and there arises between them the love that dispels despair: "I wasn't alone any more, I had found some affection in Crete... And this filled me with a strange joy..." (102).

Lefteris invites Katerina to his village, where she meets his delightful grandfather and Grandpa's special friend, Sally. As soon as she returns from this brief period of euphoria, however, Katerina faces ever worsening troubles. The townspeople have heard of her excursion and condemn it; her one friend, Froso, a local woman who is the only other female teacher at the high school, is forbidden to continue to associate with her.

Then Katerina learns that a young student has contracted tuberculosis and has been isolated in a distant hut where not even his mother is permitted to visit him. Appalled by this callousness, Katerina visits the child daily and eventually arranges for him to be accepted in a clinic in Athens. Rather than being grateful, however, the townspeople are furious at her for endangering the health and lives of the other students by violating the quarantine. Convinced that tuberculosis is incurable, and that the child should therefore be left to die in peace, they trail Katerina as she escorts the child's stretcher to the ferry headed for Athens, catcalling and hissing at her all the way. Having thus earned universal enmity in the town, Katerina finds that her relationship with Lefteris has been effectively poisoned by the negative pressure he is subjected to. The coup de grace is delivered when she takes the high school girls on the excursion to the prostitutes.

The second low point, shortly before the end of the book, occurs when the principal of the girls' high school rails at her, calling her "a moron" and an "imbecile." After he leaves the room, the young teacher begins to cry, and then follows her own principal to his house (for safety) "with her head hanging, like a student who has been reprimanded" (173).

The novel ends with Katerina sailing from Crete. Her departure is rather a relief, considering her tribulations on the island. The matter of her lover Lefteris seems more or less forgotten by then.

Personas in the Extreme

The native Cretans are broadly drawn. They are repeatedly called *fantasmenoi,* swell-headed, vain in a puffed-up way. They are magalomaniacs, overimpressed with their own importance and prowess. In contrast, Katerina habitually characterizes herself as insignificant, announcing, like Emily Dickinson, "I'm nobody." The tone is set when her boat arrives in Crete and she is "supposed to get down from the ship by a staircase that was dancing over the wild sea" (11). Rather than brave the staircase, she hides in the smoking room. As Heracles turns the boat upside down looking for her, the prospective teacher burrows deeper into the boat. This is the same cowardly pose that she takes when her students shoot it out in class and she huddles under the desk. Again, after the whorehouse excursion, Katerina is more afraid that the Superintendent will yell at her than she is of losing her job (174). She continually condemns herself: "Why was I so stupid?" (172) Yet with this mouse-like persona, she does just as she likes and manages to turn the town of Rethymnon upside down.

The narrative stance, however, makes Katerina a perfect foil to expose the townspeople's hypocrisy as well as to heighten the comic effect of her actions. Hers is truly a Christlike innocence: the tubercular child and the seedy prostitutes are equally objects of her love. As if to draw the parallel directly, Katerina rides to Lefteris' village on a gentle donkey, and her students remind her, when they present her with their going-away gift, that she often says the donkey is a blessed creature because Christ rode one. In keeping with this correspondence, the townspeople "crucify" her in the end.

Social Commentary

In Nakos's novels personal struggles are caused by social, political, and economic forces. In *Mrs. Doremi* the social forces are the hypocrisy and ignorance that reign in Rethymnon. Political concerns surface in the form of occasional references to the government's responsibility to do more for the farmers and the poor. Katerina praises the *laos,* peasants like Lefteris' grandfather, and she ridicules the superficial, money-hungry middle class, represented by her mother's Athenian relatives, Lefteris' father, and most of the people of Reythmnon. Even at school, the young teacher especially loves the little village boys who are always serious and well-behaved, while the sons of the middle class give her trouble.

Without editorial comment, Nakos presents the plight of the Cretan poor: the children who sit glumly during the first French class because they have no money to buy books, the little girl who gets up at three o'clock in the morning to begin her work in the fields and the house, the seamstresses who work for Katerina's landlady besides doing their own domestic chores, splashing water on their faces to keep themselves awake as they sew dresses for impatient ladies of the middle class. Their boss complains to Katerina: "If you only knew what I go through with them.... You open your mouth to tell them something, right away they get insulted and throw the needles in your face and leave." Nakos's comment is simply to have Katerina ask how much she pays them. The landlady admits, "It's true I don't pay them much!..." (86)

A Thirst for Freedom

The attitude of the girls who work for the landlady, despite their poverty, is typical of the Cretan temperament as it is dramatized and extolled in *Mrs. Doremi*. Whereas earlier Nakos works are primarily concerned with the search for love and the yearning to overcome painful loneliness and isolation, in contrast the perennially sought ideal in this novel is freedom. The Cretans value their freedom above all. That is why they are especially fond of naming their daughters Eleftheria ("Freedom") and their sons the masculine equivalent, Eleftherios (for which the nickname is Lefteris).

Although true Cretans love freedom, they cannot attain it any more than characters in other Nakos works achieve love. When the English artist Sally is forbidden to sit on the pier in Rethymnon in her bathing suit, she yells at the policeman, "Isn't there any freedom in this place?" (121). Katerina cannot bear the idea of loss of freedom either. In fact, when she sees a goat tied up one day, she frees it to roam unfettered with its two kids. As for herself, having been warned that she'd better watch her behavior lest she lose her job, Katerina says, "If that's what it's like to be a public servant in Greece, to live with the anxiety that they might fire you, that's tyranny, slavery!" (128)

"Tyranny" also describes a father's power over his children. This is seen, first, in Lefteris' father who hounds his son into abandoning Katerina, then invites him to his own engagement ceremony, without informing him beforehand of the proposed marriage arrangement. Katerina's fellow teacher, Froso, isn't allowed to leave her house except to go to work, nor will her father marry her off because that would deprive him of her contribution to the housework. Froso's words are reminiscent of those of Marina, the island nursemaid in *Nafsika*. Froso says,

> As for the injustice that occurs in this place against women, it can't be expressed. . . . I've felt this injustice since I was small. First I saw the preference and the love that my father showed to my brothers, because they were boys! Then he used to say: For men everything is allowed! But for the woman, he believed she has to live with chains on her legs, to be the man's slave! He said that again and again to my poor mother. In the end she believed it too and submitted. (48)

If a woman marries, she is enslaved by her husband; if she does not, she remains a slave to her father.

Given this dynamic by which women are enslaved by men, what attitude can a woman take toward people of the opposite sex? The range of possibilities is illustrated, again with comic effect, by the series of maids that the principal hires to take care of his obese wife, Andromache.

The first maid is a shepherdess who takes a swing at any man who comes near her. She leaves shortly, stealing the principal's flute when she goes (she is a music-loving as well as castrating female). Antithetically, the second maid throws herself into the arms of every man she sees. The next two maids are also opposites. The third, Argyro, is a sleepwalker who tears up the principal's books and throws them out the window in her sleep, while the fourth is still waiting for her groom because she will marry only a bookstore owner like her father, although there are no bookstores in the town. Andromache, the principal's wife, whose name means "man-battler," finally ends up with a nondescript old woman as her maid.

Sally is the only woman in *Mrs. Doremi* who manages to live freely. Since she is not Greek, Greek society does not bind her. She is married, moreover, to an Englishman who himself suggested that she go live in Crete since she loved the place so much and could not bear Athens, where he must live because of his work. Sally is the antithesis of the Greek wives who are unable to be free.[3]

Women and Men Come to Terms

While the oppression of women is mentioned in *Mrs. Doremi* along with the struggles of the poor; and while the novel depicts the impossibility of women achieving freedom; yet relationships between women and men are not the central focus of this novel as they are in *The Lost, The Deflowered One,* and *Nafsika.* The parents whose relationships are central constellations in the other works are far in the background here. Katerina's love for Lefteris is only one element in her stormy romance with Crete; it is a symbol of her love for Greek villagers. Katerina talks of planning to marry Lefteris, but her love for him does not consume her, and she is far from devastated when he fades from her life under pressure from his father.

Men and women are no longer enemies in *Mrs. Doremi.* Most of the characters in the comic world are good at heart, the men as well as the women. The principal, the Superintendent, and Lefteris' grandfather are all sympathetic characters. Lefteris is downright heroic when he protects Katerina from the other boys at school and her tormentors in town. When he eventually buckles under pressure, he is not condemned. There are, however, bad men: Lefteris' father, the principal of the girls' high school who rails at Katerina after the excursion, and the troublemaker Karderinakis, but the influence of these "bad guys" does not dominate the novel.

Even if the men who oppress them are not malicious, the women are nonetheless victims. Heracles gives Katerina an ominous introduction to Crete when he tells her about Kiki, a beautiful young French singer who fell in love with a Cretan, gave him all her money, and joined him in the mountains where she got sick and lost her voice. Heracles reports, "Now I think she's in Chania giving French lessons. But she's fallen, she got ugly. No one wants her any more, and she barely earns her living" (16). Heracles also tells Katerina about the doctor's German wife who can be seen pacing her room after dark. She too used to be beautiful:

"But she was so unhappy here she soon became unrecognizable. She lost her flesh and her beauty. You'll see—she'll die if she stays here any longer. . . . If you pass by at night you'll see her shadow behind the white curtain of the window, going and coming like a caged bird." (40)

As for her husand,

"Oh, what can he do? He's tired of her already... Anyway, he has his work. He goes to the villages to see patients or he sits in the cafe playing backgammon with his friends. Men here don't stay home to keep their wives company..." (40)

Finally, there is Andromache, the principal's wife, a former opera singer now bedridden and paralyzed by her own pathological fat. Sally has no trouble diagnosing Andromache's illness: "Do you know what it means to be an artist, a prima donna applauded nightly by the crowd, to devote yourself to your art, and then to be closed up in a house with a high school principal and become a common housewife... That's why she got sick" (125).

Since this is what it means to get married, Katerina, like Marina in *The Deflowered One* and Alexandra in *The Lost,* is saved despite herself, when she is forced to leave Crete alone. For although Lefteris truly loves Katerina, even the most broad-minded men are subject to society's pressure and transfer this oppression to women. Lefteris, for example, asks Katerina not to talk to the French Catholic priest since this gives the evil Karderinakis evidence to convince his parents she is Catholic. Katerina's connection with Lefteris is thus a bondage even though he is more honorable than the former lover she recalls (an expatriate Greek who sounds very like Kostas in *The Lost*), and he abandons her practically if not intentionally by retreating to his village to escape his parents who live in town.

A Cynical Smile

Since it is a comic novel, *Mrs. Doremi* has a humorous rather than a tragic tone. Its message, nonetheless, is similar to those of more sober Nakos works. It depicts a world in which parents and children are alienated from each other. As in *Boetian Earth* and even *Nafsika,* there is greater affinity between grandparent and grandchild, leapfrogging a generation. Lefteris and his grandfather are of a kind, associated with the village, which is an idealized representation of Greece. Katerina, by a similar principle, misses not her mother but a mother-substitute, her French governess Pauline who springs from the peasantry.

One distinctive feature of *Mrs. Doremi* is its portrayal of an ongoing Greek tragedy: Greece's inability to take advantage of the services of enlightened expatriates who have returned to their homeland. In its treatment of Katerina the town of Rethymnon is rather like the sow that eats her farrow: rather than welcoming the talents that Katerina has developed by living abroad, the townspeople are outraged at her for being different.

One of Nakos's most popular and best-known novels, *Mrs. Doremi* was reprinted in an inexpensive pocket edition in 1971. Her only comic novel, it remains a testament to Nakos's resilience in the face of personal misfortune, as well as to her versatility as a writer.

Chapter Seven
Return to Greek Roots: *Boetian Earth*

In the midst of the harrowing starvation and constant fear that Nakos depicted in the short stories of *The Children's Hell,* she found a way to escape, in her imagination, the German-occupied city of Athens. She managed to dull the hunger pains that constantly tormented her by pushing her knee into her stomach, and in this distorted position she wrote about the town of Leivadia in the province of Boetia where she had spent happy summers as a child with her paternal grandfather. The long novel that resulted was published in 1955 under the title *Anthropina Pepromena* [Human Fate] and reprinted in 1964 as *Gi Tis Voiotias* [Beotian Earth], after the title of the successful French translation (*Terre de Béotie,* Lausanne, 1962). The most recent reprint (Athens, 1978) has returned to the original title.

Together with its sequel, *Toward a New Life,* which Nakos wrote much later, and her last novel, *Ikarian Dreamers, Boetian Earth* represents Nakos's mature style. Rather than a first-person narrative, it is a third-person account in which the point of view of the main protagonist is interspersed with points of view of other characters who figure in the plot. While social injustice and class differences continue to be prominent concerns, directly political themes are developed as well. However, *Boetian Earth* is a transitional work in the sense that it is still concerned with a romantic notion of good and evil that are clearly distinguished in the characters and events.

The Story

Boetian Earth chronicles the childhood and coming of age of Barbara, the child of a once-wealthy, now-broken Athenian home, who has come to live with her paternal grandparents in the provincial town of Leivadia because her father, who was a leftist politician, has died, and her mother has remarried a man who does not want the little girl around.

Barbara's Grandma is a cold, stern woman whose main preoccupation is maintaining her home as the provincial headquarters of her brother, a conservative member of Parliament who becomes president of the legislature. Grandpa, on the other hand, is the person Barbara loves most in the world. He is gentle, generous, and humanitarian. To the delight of his granddaughter and the chagrin of his wife, he takes the little girl with him on midnight rides to the villages where he distributes what little extra grain he has to the even poorer villagers.

In her grandmother's house Barbara hangs around the kitchen with the village girls who work for Grandma in exchange for their board; she visits Grandpa in his attic room where he reads and plays the flute; she holes up in her private retreat: the hammam, a half-ruined Turkish bath-house, in the backyard; she roams the countryside with her friend Thanasis, a village boy whom Grandpa has "adopted" as his helper.

Grandpa, Thanasis, and Barbara spend much of their time with Antonina, a gentle widow who plays an instrument called a *santouri*. Shortly after the novel begins, Antonina leaves for Switzerland in order to fetch her son Andreas, who is paralyzed with congenital syphilis. During Antonina's absence, Grandpa takes Thanasis and Barbara on a trip to mountain villages, where they meet a clairvoyant nun named Sister Timothea who predicts World War I in a trancelike seizure.

After they return to Leivadia, Grandma's and Grandpa's second son, Spyros, returns from America with his Greek-American wife Evel and their daughter. At this point the story is told of how Barbara's father Loukas, an idealistic intellectual, was killed because of his activities in organizing the local workers, apparently betrayed by his sadistic brother Spyros. While Loukas was

Grandpa's favorite, Spyros is clearly allied with Grandma. As Spyros gets busy with conservative politics, his wife Evel becomes friends with Grandpa and Barbara, until Spyros takes her to live in Athens.

One day Barbara sneaks out during the hot midday siesta to spy on the neighbors' yard. She sees two strange old sisters with a bloody human fetus. Following this trauma, Barbara falls ill and languishes between life and death as Grandpa and Thanasis keep agonized vigils. Barbara recovers, waking into a new sexual self and a new relationship with Thanasis. However, at this time Antonina returns, bringing her ethereal, intellectual son Andreas, with whom Barbara develops a deep spiritual rapport.

An archeologist named Piavelis arrives in town and joins the circle of Grandpa and Antonina. When the ladies of the town ask him to give them free art appreciation lessons, the archeologist agrees. In return for his generous efforts, he is arrested and jailed, accused of such crimes as corrupting the women by showing them indecent paintings, secretly making love to his statues, and lecturing in comprehensible demotic Greek.[1] Piavelis's most vicious slanderer is a villain named Skoureas who, like Katerina's enemy Karderinakis in *Mrs. Doremi,* seems to have no motivation other than his malicious nature. Piavelis' trial ends in his acquittal thanks to the testimony of Grandma's cook who admits that Skoureas, to whom she has been secretly "engaged," forced her to write the poison-pen letters incriminating Piavelis.

The archeologist returns to his native island, Corfu, and Grandpa and Antonina take the three children to a monastery on the slopes of Mt. Parnassus. News arrives from Athens that Evel, unable to stand her husband Spyros's cruelty and the narrowness of Greek society, is returning to America.

At the monastery Barbara first spends all her time with her earthy friend Thanasis, but when Antonina's son Andreas's health takes a turn for the worse, she devotes herself entirely to him. In a jealous rage, Thanasis kills Andreas's pet canary, then runs to his village in remorse and shame. Therefore, he isn't in town when Barbara leaves Leivadia for good; her mother's second husband dies, and her mother decides to take Barbara back to live with her in Athens.

Boetian Earth dramatizes a struggle between good and evil forces which are represented by two opposing camps: one consisting of Grandma and her allies, the other headed by Grandpa. Grandma's world is associated with conservative politics. In contrast, Grandpa and his friends are concerned, not with leftist politics, but with art and other humanistic and humanitarian pursuits. These two worlds are represented by Grandma's house, on the one hand, and, on the other, the home of Grandpa's friend Antonina:

> Thus the two children, Thanasis and Barbara, were growing up in two different environments, in two houses: Grandma's and Antonina's, which didn't resemble each other in any way, even if they were so close in the same neighborhood. In one house a world moved around politics, caught up with a mania for politics. In the other, art and music were welcomed and were the adoration of all who frequented there. (235)[2]

Grandma's house is associated with Athens, since her brother and her son travel back and forth between Athens and Leivadia. Grandpa feels out of place in this environment. He either goes to visit Antonina or retreats to his attic to read and play the flute. Grandpa is more comfortable in the villages of Boetia which he visits with Barbara. He is associated with the Boetian earth of the title.

Spirits and Ghosts

Nakos is interested in spiritual phenomena. Her characters often have prophetic dreams and premonitions, and many of her works have a supernatural aura about them. This effect is particularly palpable in *Boetian Earth*, which often feels like a long fairy tale, with its talk of magic and enchantment, of spirits and ghosts.

Grandpa's American daughter-in-law Evel tells him, "You create such a warmth around yourself that it attracts people like a charm" (127). Grandma says that Antonina has "bewitched" him and Barbara (46). Antonina's son Andreas is pure spirit; he charms everyone. Besides the effect created by people's power to charm, music is characterized as a force that enchants people. When Grandpa plays the flute or Antonina plays the *santouri*, others are literally mesmerized.

The sense of the spiritual which pervades *Boetian Earth* is enhanced by the character Sister Timothea, a nun who has psychic powers. Next to her, "Barbara felt inside herself an inexplicable joy, like when she listened to Grandpa in the evening playing that wonderful melody on the flute" (94). Timothea's faith serves as Grandpa's inspiration. However, she also foretells doom, predicting World War I in a terrifyingly vivid vision of destruction.

Barbara's private hideaway, the hammam in the backyard, is an enchanted world. There she senses the words she will one day write: "And these mysterious words, which the child herself didn't yet know but searched to find, fluttered around her too like music. Of course she was still too young to express them... but they held her there, nonetheless, enchanted with a strange poignancy" (189). The hammam is "wet and deep like a well" (19), moreover, and in Nakos's books, as in Greek folklore, wells are always the homes of spirits.

Leivadia itself is a magical town. Grandpa takes Barbara out at night on his horse, as he goes to the villages to distribute food. At this hour, the town's magic is evident:

Leivadia was no longer the big village with its cobblestones, but a different, fantastic city, with towers, as in fairytales, with mysterious narrow lanes, with houses all shuttered and deserted, as if bewitched. (25)

The sense of mystery and enchantment is a force that combines the ancient as well as the folk traditions of Greece. On their way to the villages, Grandpa greets Mt. Parnassus which towers over the province of Boetia. He addresses the Muses, the daughters of Old Man Parnassus, who live there, according to ancient mythology. Thanasis objects that the mountain is not inhabited by Muses any more, but rather by fairies and other more modern spirits. Grandpa responds, "Don't you know that whether fairies or Muses live there, it's the same, and only the name has changed?... It's enough that they're there, to inspire poor humans" (47). Three chapters in particular are suffused with supernatural overtones. One is the chapter in which Barbara witnesses the bizarre scene in her neighbors' yard, which will be discussed presently. Another is the chapter in which Thanasis kills Andreas's canary as if in a trance. Grandpa and Barbara hear him on the terrace as he performs this act, but they are also bewitched, transfixed by the strains of Antonina's *santouri*, so they are unable to move to see what he's doing. After his crime Thanasis runs to his village through woods suffused with eery moonlight. He is terrified as he hears stones rolling as if pushed by an invisible spirit (346).

The part played by spirits and ghosts is presented not without humor. In the chapter entitled "Sister Timothea" Thanasis and Barbara are filled with eery feelings as they wander into a deserted church. When they hear a disembodied woman's voice begging to be unchained, they bolt in terror. However, the village women later explain that the voice came from a real person: the priest's daughter, who is indeed chained, because she has fallen in love with a spirit and keeps running off to the mountain to cavort with it. The spirit, however, turns out to be an equally real and handsome young shepherd.

The Heroic Triumvirate

The heroine of *Boetian Earth*, Barbara, has much in common with other Nakos heroines. She is innocent, sensitive, compassionate. "I feel sorry for everyone," she says. "Most of all I feel sorry for the burdened animals in the street when they're beaten ... and I feel sorry for people... I don't really know why, but I feel sorry for them" (77). In this, Barbara is reminiscent of Nafsika, another child protagonist, and *Boetian Earth* shares its fairytale atmosphere with the novella *Nafsika* as well.

Boetian Earth is unique, however, in that the heroine is bound in a close rapport of love and sympathy with two other characters, Grandpa and Thanasis, rather than being totally alienated from the people around her. In a sense, the overweening heroic figure is Grandpa (the first edition of the novel is dedicated to Nakos's grandfather), and Barbara and Thanasis represent two aspects of the old man. Grandpa is explicitly associated with old man Parnassus, who personifies the mountain which dominates the Boetian landscape. Two recurrent images intertwine: Parnassus with its snow-capped peak and Grandpa with his shock of white hair. When Grandpa confronts Piavelis' slanderers, "his snowy head stood out in the darkness of the café" (259). When he takes off his cap as a greeting to the mountain, its "white-haired head reaches above the clouds" (47). On a later trip to a monastery at the foot of the mountain Grandpa explains that no one can climb to its peak because "The white-haired old man Parnassus liked to live alone" (305), just as white-haired old Grandpa likes to be alone in his attic room. When Grandpa comes to greet Antonina, "She thought that old man Parnassus himself was coming down to meet her" (308).

Grandpa combines an impulse to escape the world with the urge to fight against injustice. When he is tormented by doubts, "He only wanted to hide like a wounded beast in his den, so he wouldn't see or hear anything until he died" (169). However, when he is enraged at Piavelis' slanderers, he rushes to confront them in the local café, shaking his cane at them and telling them off.

While Barbara and Thanasis both have Grandpa's concern for people and his love of music and books, Barbara embodies his escapist tendencies, and Thanasis has the instinct to fight. Thanasis wants to gather the people from his village to stone those who are falsely accusing Piavelis, the archeologist. His dream is to become a judge, so he can right the wrongs he sees. "I'm going to become a judge," he tells Barbara, "a judge of the world and of all society! . . . Because from the time I became aware of myself, I saw injustice in the world" (334).

Barbara's plans for their future are more escapist: "We'll come back later and buy a piece of land and cultivate it, you and I. That's what I like. I love the land. Never mind everybody else!" Moreover, Barbara continually hides out in her hammam just as

Grandpa locks himself in his attic. Barbara is a reincarnation of Grandpa's deepest impulses; when she must leave Leivadia in the end, the separation from Grandpa is "like splitting one and the same flesh" (356), for she is "flesh of his flesh" (363). Thanasis reflects a part of Grandpa in that both are part of the Boetian earth itself. If Grandpa is the mountain, Thanasis "was also a piece of the Boetian earth" (358).

The Facts of Life in a Dreamworld

Boetian Earth is, first and foremost, Barbara's story, and Grandpa and Thanasis are important because of their significance to her. The novel reflects Barbara's view of the world and her development. The episode in which she sees two neighbor women with a fetus constitutes a rude introduction to the facts of life for Barbara, just as a similar experience functions for the protagonist Marina in the early story, "The Nameless One." As Barbara becomes aware of her sexual nature, she not surprisingly expresses her sexuality with her friend Thanasis, but she does not come to terms with these impulses in *Boetian Earth*. The integration of sexuality into her life remains to be accomplished in the sequel to this novel, *Toward a New Life,* but the process is advanced farther in *Boetian Earth* than it is in any of Nakos's previous writing.

Barbara's epiphany occurs, as does Alexandra's in *The Lost,* during the spookily quiet and oppressively hot noon hours. Alexandra comes upon an objectification of her sexuality in the form of a lusty satyr carved on an ancient tomb. Barbara can expect a similar confrontation: "Porfyra and the gardener had told her that these are the hours when satyrs roam, half goats and half men, and kidnap little girls..." (156). During this portentous time of day Barbara climbs a tree overlooking the neighboring yard. Her head is burning from the heat. In keeping with the ambivalence toward sex that characterizes Barbara's attitudes, the fetus episode is enacted by two sisters, one evil and one angelic. In contrast, the short story "The Nameless One" portrays a monolithically negative attitude toward sexuality; in that story, the heroine Marina was shown her mother's fetus by a spiteful maid.

One of Barbara's neighbors, the sister Argyro, is like an evil witch. It is she who performed the abortion that resulted in the bloody fetus. The other sister, Zoe, however, is a good soul (her name means "life") who has lost her mind because of an abortion she had been forced to undergo when she was young. Mistaking the present unborn child for her own, she croons to it and gives it a little funeral.

When Barbara miraculously recovers from the grave illness she suffers following this experience, she is no longer a little girl, but an adolescent:

Frequently, lately, her head felt heavy. Her whole body burned as if she had fever, but her hands stayed ice cold...... She was impatient to live, but then she was afraid of life. Joy and sadness, dreams and melancholy, sweet like sweet wine, all these feelings together struggled with each other in her adolescent soul... Without any significant cause, tears came to her eyes, and then laughter, uncontrolled, almost hysteria. (237)

In the middle of this crazy time Barbara gets her period for the first time. She is sitting alone in her hammam when:

Suddenly she felt between her legs something flowing hot and wet like blood...
When she stood up, she saw big drops of blood on the down... On one leg in fact there was still a little red stream running... She was frightened! She was frightened, even though she realized right away what it was... She knew from the maids... She had often heard them talking... nevertheless the blood, such a deep red, frightened her...
. . .
She said to herself: Well!... So that's the whole thing?... I've become a woman, I know!... But that's how it comes, like a sickness? (239)

Despite her mixed emotions, Barbara is not repulsed by her menstrual blood. The experience, in fact, brings her closer to Thanasis.

Thanasis finds Barbara soon after she discovers the blood, and, although he does not immediately know what accounts for the change, he finds his young friend bewitchingly attractive. She bids him sit beside her and put his hand on her forehead, to feel how hot she is.

> Never before had Thanasis come so close to Barbara... Not even in his most secret dream had he imagined this... And look now, that this unbelievable miracle had come to pass!... His hand touching Barbara!... A strange trembling seized him, and inside him it was as if his soul shivered from emotion. (240)

When she stands up to leave, Barbara remembers the blood on her skirt. Although she is embarrassed, she has no trouble confiding in Thanasis: "It seems I've become a real woman!..." Thanasis, too, is moved rather than repelled:

> This mystery captivated him, but at the same time it filled his soul with awe, as if he were seeing the hatching of a chrysalis which throws off its silk cocoon and, drunk from the light, begins to fly, to begin a new, different life. Yes, the boy felt as if he had witnessed one of the mysteries of nature. (241)

This shared experience becomes a bond between Barbara and Thanasis: "From that day the two children felt that they were more closely bound to each other." This bond is in stark contrast to the heightened alienation that Marina experiences in "The Nameless One." After her traumatic introduction to the facts of life by the double trauma of seeing her unborn brother and also being molested by her mother's lover, Marina cannot share her emotions with anyone. She wanders alone by the shore, and when her friends try to approach, she throws rocks at them.

Despite Barbara's promising, even romantic, introduction to her sexual nature, she is torn between her physical attraction to Thanasis and her platonic love for the ethereal, bedridden Andreas. Thanasis represents a literally "earthy" attraction: "Thanasis' strong, peasant body made of the soil of the Boetian earth, pulled her own body strangely, like a magnet, and inside her a heap of longings awoke, which she herself couldn't yet sort out" (331). In contrast, Andreas represents the soul: "Everything in him was pure and his feelings ethereal. Nothing fleshly drew the girl to Andreas. It was a pure love, deep and spiritual" (331).

Thanasis surmises, correctly, that Barbara cannot reconcile these two forces within herself. He tells her, "Now that I'm growing up I understand, Barbara, that in order to be complete, love wants the body as well as the soul. You're looking sometimes for one and sometimes the other, and you separate them" (316). Barbara and Thanasis begin to kiss each other and embrace in the woods, but Barbara is hounded by guilt. Thanasis argues:

"Don't you want to come walk in the woods with me any more?"
"No, I don't want to any more! I won't go again!... it won't do for us to kiss each other like lunatics."
"And why won't it do?"
"It's wrong..."
"And why? Is love a bad thing?" Thanasis asked.
"Love isn't a bad thing. Agreed! But our crazy kissing, that's bad," Barbara answered him, always laughing. (333)

When Andreas's physical condition suddenly worsens, Barbara's guilt makes her feel responsible: "She was thinking that maybe Andreas was suffering all this, because God wanted to punish her, because she wasn't virtuous and did crazy things with Thanasis..." (337). Barbara therefore stops seeing Thanasis and spends all her time by Andreas's bedside, with the result that Thanasis takes jealous revenge on Andreas's canary, and then retreats to his village, so that Barbara never sees him again in this novel. In this sense the novel ends with Barbara tilting toward the asexual bond she has with Andreas. If Thanasis is the earth, Andreas is the sky, which he talks about at length and felt so close to in the Swiss sanatorium: "I never felt bad, I had the sky before me" (199).

Marriages Made in Hell

Along with the unresolved view of sexuality, the pessimistic view of marriage which has been seen in Nakos's early work recurs in *Boetian Earth*. The central couple, from whom all the other dichotomies spiral out, are Grandma and Grandpa. Grandma is a traditionalist, with a passion for hateful politics and an indifference to human suffering. Grandpa, a humanitarian and musician, feels like a stranger in her house. She has no use for his values and his friends. Even though they have been married for so many years, Grandma and Grandpa share little mutual understanding and less mutual sympathy. All the other couples in the novel are similarly mismatched. Barbara's villainous uncle, Spyros, is married to Evel, a sympathetic character who becomes Grandpa's special friend. Barbara's father Loukas was an idealist like Grandpa, but her mother Christina is a superficial Athenian society lady. Antonina's first husband was a dissolute sadist. Her second husband was a good man, but death snatched him from her in short order.

Marriage in *Boetian Earth* is mostly a business of contrivance and disappointment. This is seen in numerous sub-plots as well as in the lives of the main characters. For example, the priest's daughter who was chained in the church is pregnant by her shepherd lover. When Grandpa learns that the shepherd does not intend to marry her, he erupts in one of his rare fits of anger, finding the shepherd and railing at him:

Listen here... on the day of Saint Constantine you'll come to the village and I'll marry you to Mariyo, the priest's daughter... and if by chance you run away to the mountains and refuse, you know—you know very well, even if you are my godchild... I'll turn you in to the authorities for that sheep theft I know about. Do you understand me? I saved you from jail once, and that was for your poor dead father's sake, but that's over and done with now, now you have to deal with me... scoundrel! (54)

A common paradox lurks here. Grandpa knows the young shepherd to be a scoundrel, yet he forces him to marry the priest's daughter. Being married to a scoundrel is better than facing the consequences of being an unwed mother.

The lesson of what can happen to a woman who does not marry the man who impregnates her is dramatized in the character Zoe, the neighbor whom Barbara watches from a tree. Zoe had been in love with a shepherd too, but her friend was a good, handsome, and even wealthy young man. But Zoe's small-minded brother refused to permit the marriage, even though he himself didn't have enough money to give her a dowry to marry someone he considered worthy of his station. The brother took Zoe to Athens to have an abortion which left her half paralyzed and entirely deranged. Money is often at the root of marriage arrangements. The archeologist Piavelis remarks sadly that he was victimized because the townspeople are all frustrated, deprived of love. Antonina responds in surprise that they are all married. The archeologist explains, "Don't you know that most marriages in today's society are arranged, a mercantile proposition in which only property and dowries are considered" (297). The novel contains abundant examples of people marrying for money. For example, the villain Skoureas, Piavelis slanderer, promises for years to marry the cook but finally decides on a more lucrative match. His affair with the cook, moreover, is another striking mismatch, for she is one of the best women in the novel, and he is one of the worst men.

The Lot of Women

All of society suffers from the institution of marriage, but women suffer most, for they are the bartered goods in the business proposition. It is not the dowry system that comes in for attack, but family pressure on a woman, as was seen in Zoe's case, to make a marriage that will be of use to them socially or economically. Thus Antonina's mother pushed her to marry her dreadful first husband: "Marry him! He's a good man... he has a lot of money... He'll take care of your father, who lost his job in the municipal government. He'll take care of your brothers and find them jobs. Why don't you take pity on us?" (39)

When Spyros's Greek-American wife Evel returns with her husband to his native Greece, she is in for a shock when he starts treating her as he would a Greek wife. He sneers at her, "What do you think, that we're in America, where women do as they please? We're in Greece, and now I have you in my net!" (136). Evel, however, refuses to play the role. She speaks up:

> I can't understand why women here in the provinces sit closed in their houses. They're crocheting lace, they say, for their trousseau... I see

them behind closed windows... and if a groom isn't found, then what do they do? They wither away. Why don't they rise up and throw off the tyranny of the father, the brother, and the mother-in-law? (119)

Unable to live her own life in Greece, Evel eventually returns to the United States.

Like many of the best Nakos women, Evel is androgynous. She is boyish. When she arrives wearing culottes, the maids are aghast to see a woman wearing pants. Taking off her hat, she shocks them even more: "She had her hair cut short, and her whole head was covered with tiny curls like a little boy's" (57). She insists on riding a horse, straddling it like a man. The servant girl Kalomoira remarks with disdain, "She's like a boy. One time I happened to touch her arm; it's hard like a man's" (120).

Evel teaches Barbara gymnastics and awakens her to sensual appreciation of her own body. Barbara feels freer wearing the bathing suit Evel gives her. But as soon as Evel leaves, Grandma forbids Barbara to wear the bathing suit, to shower herself in the backyard, to swing from the gymnastic bars that Evel had had built. Grandma thinks girls should stay indoors and learn to cook and sew. This is particularly ironic since Grandma herself had wanted to be educated but had to give up her hopes to go to work so her brothers could study. Grandma is frustrated: "I have my mind on work, on serious matters, and on politics; it's only a pity God made me a woman; I wouldn't sit like Grandpa playing the flute and not seeing anyone" (190). Yet Grandma imposes the same frustration on her grandchild.

Barbara is saved because Grandpa believes women should be educated and have independent careers, as the mother in *Nafsika* believes. The mother in *Boetian Earth* has quite different visions of her daughter's future. She wants Barbara to become a lady-in-waiting at the palace.

The most heroic female character in this novel is the cook, who is also androgynous. She has a gruff, masculine voice; she tells dirty jokes; she is large. Nearly always called "the moustached cook," she is the only one courageous enough to stand up in court and speak in defense of the archeologist, Piavelis. When she does this, she is said to "reign." The cook is unusual in that she is aligned with neither Grandma nor Grandpa. When the maids gossip in the kitchen she defends everyone who is unjustly slandered. The word *mageirissa,* "cook," is similar to the word *mageissa,* "witch," and the cook is indeed like a good witch. She knows everything about everyone and exorcises evil spirits. She is even a friend of the neighbor Zoe, who also seems like a white witch.

Boetian Earth is controlled by a series of dichotomies: good and evil, male and female, spirit and flesh. The cook is a unifying principle. When she is testifying in court, the narrator comments, "Beneath this vast bosom, who knows what primeval passions of hate and love struggle with each other!" (277). Although she is the lover of Skoureas, the arch-villain, and even helped him in his villainous work, the cook is good, and her good triumphs in the end.

Although it clearly presents women as oppressed and exploited, *Boetian Earth* is not feministic in the contemporary sense. While economic equality is certainly a goal, Nakos does not question many aspects of the way in which males and females have traditionally related to each other. Antonina, for example, does nothing but sit in her house and entertain her son and her friends. When the men have their endless discussions in her house, she sits by, listening and knitting. Moreover, Grandpa is extremely protective of her. When he hears in court that a woman is about to take the stand in Piavelis' behalf, rather than being glad, he is afraid that the woman will turn out to be Antonina. He would not wish her to compromise herself, even in such a worthy cause.

Thanasis takes a similar stance toward Barbara, and the narrative endorses it. When Barbara has begun to menstruate, Thanasis experiences suddenly "a sense of affection and protectiveness combined... The kind feeling of the male toward the female, since nature made him stronger" (241). But even if it is not revolutionary in a contemporary sense, *Boetian Earth* is deeply concerned with the state of women, deploring the injustice they suffer, and the difficulty and hopelessness of their lives. The young village girls work like slaves for Grandma in hopes that she will one day give them dowries and find them husbands, although there is doubt she will in fact do this. The cook, for example, is thirty-five and still waiting. Nevertheless, they prefer this life to what they would have had in store had they stayed in their villages. That prospect can be seen in Thanasis' mother who is so exhausted when she goes to bed at night that her body writhes and twitches while she sleeps.

Social and Political Dimensions

The servant girls, and women in general, are portrayed as oppressed. So too are the poor villagers and the workers at the local factory. In a larger sense, everyone is oppressed by the backward social institutions and the corrupt political system.

The politics of Grandma, her brother the President of the Legislature, and her son Spyros are a reminder of this system. Grandpa scorns politics. While his dead son Loukas (Barbara's father) was active in proletarian causes, Grandpa is enraged when Spyros implies his brother Loukas had been aligned with the Communist Party: "My son never worked for any Party! He died for an Idea!" (64) This is not to say, however, that Grandpa lacks political conviction. He is full of passionate intensity in his hatred of the conservative old-line politics and in support of the leftist democrat, Venizelos. It is rather the worst characters who lack all conviction, for they are only interested in the power and glory of politics, not the ideas behind it.

Grandma's house is always filled with visiting townspeople and villagers who troop to the house of the President of the Legislature and are his faithful constituency, not because they believe in his policies—they don't!—but because he has power in Athens, and they must pay with their votes in order to gain his favors when they need to get anything done. He, in turn, to keep their votes, helps them circumvent government bureaucracy in their personal business matters, instead of pursuing reforms that would really improve their lot.

The hardheartedness of the conservative party is summed up by Grandma's indifference to the exploitation of workers in the local textile plant. Barbara is upset when she hears weeping and shouting from the window of the prison-like factory building.

Thinking of the eight-year-old children who work from morning until evening for twenty-five cents a day, she asks her grandmother what is going on inside. Grandma scoffs, "It's nothing. The forewoman must be yelling at the workers and beating the children" (29). Grandma's passion for politics does not entail any sense of responsibility in social matters.

Barbara and Thanasis do feel responsible. Just before she leaves Leivadia in the end, Barbara looks at the factory and thinks of the inhumane treatment of its workers, recalling Thanasis' plan to deliver justice when he grows up. Personal and social injustice are linked in the narrative, for the hearse-like car that comes to take Barbara away appears "from the corner where the factory was" (370). Barbara is wrenched from her beloved Grandpa and from the healthy rural environment of Leivadia, in order to return to her selfish and frivolous mother and a drab life locked in an Athens apartment. The resultant suffering is equally deep for Barbara, who is thus uprooted, and for Grandpa, who is left desolate.

The novel ends, then, in a vision of social injustice represented by the factory with its oppressed workers and the sinister encroachment of industrialization on the agricultural province. This factory resembles a prison because economic hardship destroys freedom as ruthlessly as political oppression.

The Search for Freedom

Boetian Earth, like other Nakos novels, decries all forces that limit human freedom. Besides the economic hardship suffered by workers, and the personal loss of freedom by women who are controlled by their families in their choice of husbands, in the social sphere a constant preoccupation with what people will say, a fear of being made *rezili,* ridiculous, constitutes a form of imprisonment.

Furthermore, the family itself can imprison, as Evel learns when she arrives in Greece: "Suddenly she felt that she had come alone, like a dumb bird, to be caught in the invisible net. The net of the Greek family, which often chokes its own children with its backwardness" (116).

Finally, and most important, there is the underlying dilemma that Grandpa confronts, the inescapable imprisonment of the soul in the body:

And Grandpa's soul was in turmoil; it knocked against the bars of a dark prison, the prison of the flesh. He struggled to see the light but his eyes were dimmed by the darkness of the flesh; for years now... he struggled to free himself and he couldn't. (169)

This conflict can be seen metaphorically in discussions about the canary which the abbot in the monastery "Jerusalem" gives to the paralyzed child Andreas:

"Don't feel sorry for him, my boy, because he's locked in the cage," the abbot said to him, "because he doesn't mind. He was born in the cage and he doesn't know freedom, so he can't miss it..." This made a great impression on Thanasis, however, who happened to be there when the abbot said this, and he remained thoughtful for a long time. (323)

The canary becomes the symbol for imprisonment on several levels. On the most concrete level the caged bird reminds people of real jails. Piavelis remarks when he is released that he can't even bear to see "a bird imprisoned in a cage" (293). On a deeper level the bird represents each person's isolation. Antonina refers to this when she comments, "Sometimes one wants to forget that we too are like the canary inside the cage" (303).

Andreas likes the bird because it was born caged, as he was born caged in his paralyzed body. It is fitting that the canary belongs to him, moreover, because Andreas loves the sky, and he is, in a way, a pure spirit. When Thanasis kills the canary out of jealousy, he is expressing his resentment against the pure spirit which Barbara prefers when she chooses Andreas's company over the earthy love Thanasis offers her. Perhaps this is why Thanasis is disturbed by the abbot's argument that the canary does not mind his cage. Thanasis believes that people must grip and shake the bars of their prisons.

Sensing their imprisonment, the heroes and heroines of *Boetian Earth* experience a longing for escape both in the temporary form of a private retreat and in the impulse to travel far. Just as Barbara has her hammam and Grandpa his attic, so Evel constructs a lofty perch for herself in a tree (in keeping with the "dumb bird" image applied to her). The ultimate withdrawal may be Sister Timothea's to the monastery, but almost as total is Piavelis' withdrawal into the study of ancient art.

The characters of this novel also long to escape geographically. Barbara experiences such a longing when listening to Grandpa give Thanasis a geography lesson. Elsewhere, Antonina's feet are a metaphor: "They were small, almost childlike little white feet, that were always moving. As if they were always looking for someplace to leave for, somewhere to go" (33). Bedridden in a Swiss sanatorium, Andreas memorized the schedules of the trains he could hear. "I knew exactly which train was passing and where it was going," he tells Barbara. ". . . then I followed them with my imagination and traveled with them" (197).

When Barbara points out a cloud in the sky and tells Thanasis, "See, it's like a little boat. How I wish I were inside it!" her friend disagrees with her: "No! I wouldn't want to be there... I'm fine right here, near you, on the earth. I love our earth here... Why do you always have a mania for wanting to be somewhere other than where you are?" (316) Thanasis is quite right in his observation about Barbara. However, he himself escapes in reading. So all the good characters need to escape, as if the world is too much with them, too much for them, even though the escapes are temporary or illusory.

In *Boetian Earth* one way out which does not exist is expatriation. This is in contrast to other works: Marina in *The Deflowered One* leaves for France, the father in *The Lost* goes to Egypt, the mother in *Nafsika* takes off for Marseilles. People in the present novel have traveled abroad: Grandpa and Piavelis studied in Italy, Antonina lived in Budapest, and Andreas spent years in Switzerland. But they have all come home. Even Spyros has come back from America. As the novel ends, moreover, all the characters return to the places of their births: Piavelis to Corfu, Evel to America, Thanasis to his village, and Barbara to her mother's home in Athens.

Embracing Hellenism

Written during the German Occupation, *Boetian Earth* reflects the preoccupation with "Greekness" which Thomas Doulis documents in his study of the novelist Theotokas.[3] In the same vein, as part of an interview with three contemporary Greek prose-writers, N. C. Germanacos observes,

> It seems to me that one of the major psychological problems facing a Greek writer—and the one that sets him clearly apart from his western colleagues—is coming to terms with what I call "the awful burden of the past." The questions: Who am I? What am I? do not trouble a Greek as much as the question: Who and what am I in the geographical space and historical time that I occupy, and what relation have I to the men who occupied this space before me?[4]

This is precisely the question that Nakos tackles in *Boetian Earth*.

For the first time in her longer fiction, the heroine has not lived abroad and will not live abroad. Longings for Paris, feelings of being a foreigner in Greece have no place in this novel. Nakos is now investigating what it means to be Greek in Greece, in terms of, as Germanacos says, geography and history.

Geographically, the setting, Boetia, is crucial to the work. As Marcel Brion observes in his introduction to the French edition, the Boetian earth itself is the real hero.[5] Thanasis and Grandpa, the idealized characters, are repeatedly represented as being parts of this earth. In his role as archeologist, Piavelis continually talks about Greece's ancient heritage and its relationship to modern Greece.

Both Grandpa and Piavelis are fond of remarking that the modern Greeks are a reincarnation of their ancient forebears, only misshapen by poverty. Grandpa says,

> Yes, we're the same! We have the same love of freedom, the same sense of honor, the same sense of hospitality and love of strangers. And if one day this people gets its fill of bread, and if eons of poverty don't eat it up, . . . this people will become great again. (230)

One day a statue is unearthed at Piavelis' excavation.

As soon as Barbara saw it—forgetting the centuries that separated them—she shouted: "Hey, it's the beggar, the old man with the bald head and ragged clothes, who begs barefoot near here, on the bridge." Everybody laughed, but the workers thought so too and said the same thing. Only Grandpa and the archeologist didn't laugh but were moved. They both knew well that it really was the same beggar, even if he had been born some centuries earlier. They knew well that that people and this were the same. . . . (230)

The adoration of Greece in *Boetian Earth* is inspired not only by ancient history but also by recent history. Stratis Tsirkas, one of the best modern Greek novelists, pointed out the great impact of the 1821 Revolution in which Greece first successfully liberated itself from Turkish rule. Tsirkas noted, "But the war itself, the revolution, as we call it in Greek, created a new mythology, which the Greek people fell back on when the time came for them to fight again for their independence. They did not refer to ancient Greece when the resistance was formed against the Germans, when the whole guerilla movement began. Our ideal then was 1821."[6]

Accordingly, the Revolution of 1821 is a recurrent theme in *Boetian Earth*, which was written during that time of resistance against the Germans. Repeated reference is made to the fact that Grandpa's family were heroes of the Revolution, to which they gave all their money, and in which Grandpa's father and brother lost their lives. Grandpa proclaims, "And I consider it an honor to be poor, that last of a generation that gave its life and its wealth to the great struggle, thanks to whom you are free men today, gentlemen, and not vassals of the Turks as before!" (159–60). A faithful old gardener gives a similar lecture to the young women who work in the kitchen: "Look, don't you know the old noblemen were made to scatter their wealth, to be *levendes*, and Grandpa is a *levendis*, but instead of having guns, he now has the flute and books!" (12).[7]

As if to preserve the "goodness" of the image of the Greek provinces, Nakos has Grandpa knowingly assert that Piavelis' slanderers are not locals but outsiders. However, this parochial suspicion of Greeks from other places, although it faithfully reflects a prejudice which was common against Asia Minor refugees, is not the message of the book as a whole. The abbot in the monastery, who is from Sozopol, Bulgaria, delivers a moving speech about Panhellenism:

"The Greek forgets where he came from, the old cradle of nobility... We at least, who lived with the Greeks of the Pontus, on the Black Sea, who also knew Hellenism, we learned to feel for and love not only our fatherland, in the narrow sense, but Hellenism as a whole. Greece for us wasn't just a piece of land. It was her tradition, her civilization, which you found spread all over Anatolia... But now, especially the youth who don't know these things very well, they forget... (324)

Grandpa agrees that, paradoxically, the fatherland itself threatens rather than nurtures Hellenism, by promoting a narrow view of it and by stunting the minds of its children in school:

But from the time Greece became a so-called organized state, all this is being lost... You see they made schools to twist children up... Instead of enriching their souls, they make them memorize syntax, and they even make the ancient writers... unrecognizable, 'til you get sick of them for good! (324)

Thus this novel continues to bewail the ways in which Greece makes her own children suffer. Nonetheless, *Boetian Earth* represents the beginning of Nakos's reconciliation with her homeland, idealizing Hellenism and reclaiming from its past a sense of strength and pride.

Just as Grandpa triumphs over his doubts when he is brought near despair contemplating "the indifference of the universe," borne in upon him by the threat of Barbara's death, so the entire novel represents Nakos's personal struggle to maintain her faith despite the overwhelming suffering of everyone around her during the German Occupation.

Chapter Eight
Political Bitterness and Personal Hope: *Toward a New Life*

Lilika Nakos sits outside a little white house in Ekali, about a forty-five minute ride from Athens. Fashionable suburban estates have sprung up around her family's old country home, now hopelessly rundown, which according to a literary critic "was a constant center of hospitality for Greek and foreign . . . literati and friends of literature."[1] Now it hosts only Nakos herself, the young women from Ikaria who visit and help her, and occasional close friends. The house is set back from the road, surrounded by pine trees which have dropped their cones and needles onto the ground. Nakos and I are sitting on the porch, as she tells me how she came to write one of her novels.

"I wrote *Yia Mia Kainouryia Zoi* [Toward a New Life] when I was roused against the Metaxas dictatorship," Nakos recalls, referring to the oppressive dictator Ioannis Metaxas who ruled Greece between 1936 and 1941. At that time, she says, she was teaching at the Eighth Boys' High School in Athens, where the principal cooperated with the security police and tormented and denounced the working-class students as Communists. Then Nakos talks of a friend named Chrysa.

She was a seamstress before, and then she joined the Party, the Communists, and organized in factories. She came to our house often. I loved her. Not that I was a Communist—I didn't get involved—but my mother felt sorry for her too. She was a very nice girl. . . . Anyway, she believed in a better life. That one day the world would change. . . .

Someone went to the police. He wanted to make her his, to sleep with her. She didn't want to. And he turned her in. He had her arrested. She was wearing a coat my mother had given her. They beat her to make her tell which lady had given it to her. The poor girl didn't tell. . . . She was badly beaten. They tortured her. How do I know this? I put on a kerchief and old clothes, like a worker, and they brought her and she said to me, "Lilika, if I asked for you, it's not to tell you what I went through, but for you to see what the Greek people go through. I'm a little ant. This little ant will expand to change the life of working people." I was crying. She said, "Don't cry." I said, "What did they do to you?" She said, "I'm going to die, I know."

They had turned her upside down and beat her, stuffing her slip into her mouth to muffle her screams. Then a woman burned her sexual organs with a match. Yet to Nakos,

"Don't cry, don't cry. I am," she said, "a little ant. And I sent for you because you write and you writers have a duty (that's how she spoke: *grafiades*) to know what the Greek people go through." And then they took her away and after that I learned that she died five days later. But it made a great impression on me, and I wanted to put her life and her name somewhere.

Years after the death of Chrysa and the other events of the Metaxas dictatorship, and after the ordeal of World War II,[2] Nakos created a place to put her martyred friend's life and name (though not the details of her torture), and to put many of the events of her own experience, including her dismissal from the high school where she taught and her working environment at the newspaper. She fashioned these events into the novel *Toward a New Life,* a sequel to *Boetian Earth,* fictionalizing the situations and characters into an authentic portrayal of the Metaxas era. Because of its political nature, the novel was not published until 1960, and even then, its author was harassed as a result (the rightest democratic government was still committed to preserving a lenient view of Metaxas and an unfavorable view of his Communist opponents).

At the same time that it presents a disturbing portrait of political reality, *Toward a New Life* is one of Nakos's most optimistic works, suffused with Chrysa's faith in the better life which gives the work its title. Furthermore, the novel exhibits a romanticism about love which is seen in none of Nakos's earlier works. The threads of political oppression and personal romance intertwine to make this one of Nakos's most important and successful novels. It is, above all, a pained lament for the endless suffering of Greeks who cast off the Turkish yoke only to take on native tyrants.

The Story

Toward a New Life finds Barbara, the child protagonist of *Boetian Earth*, grown up and living with her mother in Athens. Like the heroines of *The Lost* and *Mrs. Doremi,* Barbara is now responsible for supporting her aristocratic but destitute mother, Christina, who is incapable of doing anything for herself. Barbara and her mother live in the downstairs flat of a house owned by Christina's brother-in-law Pelopidas, a pathologically stingy university professor whose life is ruled by his "microbophobia": an obsessive fear of germs. Pelopidas lives in the upstairs flat, where he keeps the shutters closed and permits no one to enter except Christina, who helps him clean. However, before entering his apartment, she is required to bathe in alcohol, as he himself does. Barbara's own room is an attic retreat reminiscent of Grandpa's attic in *Boetian Earth*.

Barbara supports herself and her mother by teaching music at a boys' high school. She loves the poor children but hates the school system which oppresses rather than enlightens them. However, her career as a teacher ends abruptly when the malicious high school principal falsely denounces her as a Communist. In this state of fear and apprehension Barbara receives a note calling her to visit Victoria, the sister of Marinos, a science teacher at the high school who is also a highly accomplished astronomer completing his life's work on a book that makes astronomy comprehensible to the people, written in demotic Greek. His sister Victoria, a tireless champion of the rights of all underdogs, has the nickname *Amesos Dikaiosyni* ("Swift Justice") because she is in the habit of administering immediate corporal punishment to anyone she sees acting unjustly. Victoria has heard of Barbara's trouble, offers her friendship and support, and introduces her to a young woman who also becomes Barbara's close friend: a dedicated Communist named Chrysa.

The chapter in which Barbara goes to the police headquarters is entitled "The First Circle of Hell." Barbara spends the day sitting in the dark, cold hall with countless other innocent people, some of whom have been waiting for days, even weeks, for their interrogations. They are tormented periodically by a sadistic and deformed dwarf named Polyphemos. For example, on discovering that a kind old man has with him a trained white mouse in a cage which is his sole companion as well as his only source of income, the dwarf lifts the little mouse as if to caress it, and instead breaks its neck.

Barbara is called before the Chief of Police late in the day. His threats, however, are cut short by a phone call, and he dismisses Barbara into the courtyard. There she discovers Victoria, who arranged for her release by convincing Barbara's Uncle Spyros to intervene. This is the same Spyros who was a villain in *Boetian Earth*, now appropriately a high official in the fascist government. When Victoria sees the dwarf again harassing the old man, she snatches the dwarf up, gives him a good shaking, and dunks him headfirst into a well.

Despite her escape from the police, Barbara is left with no means of support, and she and her mother literally go hungry until her childhood friend Thanasis appears. The earthy village boy has grown up, travelled, and become an active Communist. He arranges for Barbara to work as a translator for a newspaper. The childhood romance is renewed, and Thanasis takes to visiting Barbara secretly at night in her attic room because her mother Christina would never approve of him as a friend for her daughter. The love affair between Barbara and Thanasis is paralleled by a delightfully unlikely yet successful match between Victoria and Pelopidas, the crabby recluse living in the flat above Barbara and her mother.

Thanasis is sent away from Athens on an unidentified Party mission. Victoria finds a poor servant child bound and beaten, a bad omen that signals the denouement: a rapid succession of misfortunes reminiscent of the series of disasters in the second half of *The Lost*. Both Barbara's friend Chrysa and Victoria's saintly brother Marinos, the astronomer, are arrested; Barbara disguises herself as a worker to visit what's left of Chrysa after her torture; Victoria abandons her work as a midwife to devote herself to vain efforts to free her brother.

The total derangement of the world and the bizarre nature of events in it are reflected in a story recounted at this point. There appear in the newspaper office where Barbara works a beautiful mute girl and a lascivious older woman posing as her mother who accuses the newspaper owner of having abused the girl. The woman says that he and his friends got the girl senselessly drunk, then dressed her in a bridal gown, laid her in a coffin, and staged her bawdy funeral, the newspaper owner playing the bishop with a metal vase on his head for a mitre. Immediately after hearing this story, Barbara is called out of the office and told of Chrysa's death in prison. Nothing more is said of the mute girl and her mock funeral.

Events in Athens continue to worsen. Barbara goes to Chrysa's house and finds the landlady crying because her own husband has just been arrested, too. On her way back Barbara meets a former student who tells her that the principal of the high school, in collusion with the local priest (recalling the perversion of roles of the mock funeral), has denounced most of the older students as Communists. The coup is delivered when they smell smoke. At Victoria's house, Marinos's entire life's work in astronomy is being burned as the police toss manuscripts and books out the window into a fire and smash his precious telescope.

When Victoria learns of these events, she accosts the Minister of Security in the street and brings her umbrella down on his head. The only result, however, is that he claps her under house arrest and publicizes the incident as proof of his leniency. In the meantime, Barbara's mother witnesses the collapse of her illusions. Her only hope for the future has been that Barbara will marry the nephew of an admiral. At last the admiral brings his aristocratic nephew to the house. Not only does the young man boldly announce that he intends to marry for money, but he asks Barbara to rent her lovely attic room to him as a secret meeting place for himself and his married mistress.

If this were the end, the message of the novel would be sober indeed, and it would be consonant with the tone of Nakos's early work. Instead, the narrative noses skyward once more. The professor, Pelopidas, succeeds in getting permission for Victoria to serve her house arrest on his large estate outside Athens where he marries her. In the next chapter Thanasis returns, completing the parallel charts of the two affairs, and spends an entire night with Barbara in her attic. The novel ends in exhilaration: Greece has entered the war on the side of the Allies, a move which prompts Thanasis (like many Greek citizens at the time) to forgive the dictatorship its crimes. Before leaving for battle, he asks and receives Christina's approval of his engagement to Barbara. The two young people, hand in hand, join a spontaneous street march, as Barbara proudly determines to make her own contribution to the war while waiting for Thanasis' return.

The Structure of the Novel

Toward a New Life is characterized by Nakos's accustomed structure, reflecting sharp swings of fortune, with overwhelming disaster followed finally by a hopeful ending.

The short chapter in the beginning of the novel entitled "Barbara's Kingdom" describes the lovely dreamworld of Barbara's attic room, somewhat like the short periods of happiness at the beginning of *The Lost* and *Nafsika*. Immediately after this chapter, however, Barbara is called into the principal's office and confronted with his accusation, marking the onset of her ordeal.

The low ebb in Barbara's spiritual development occurs in the middle of the book when she and her mother suffer from starvation following her ouster from the high school. Barbara's reaction to this difficult situation is to dip into a characteristic period of withdrawal:

Her old tendency[3] to dream, "to escape," as psychologists today call it, overcame her again, and with great intensity. She preferred to remain sprawled on the bed in her little attic and dream with her eyes open that she was traveling, rather than go down into the streets and run around looking for work!... Just as when she was a little girl she used to dream for hours, closed up inside her half-ruined hammam in the old house in Leivadia, so it was now... (174)

At this time Victoria happens to be away from Athens; no one else sets foot in the fallen house; mother and daughter are totally abandoned and isolated. Barbara develops the technique that Nakos reports having discovered for herself during the German Occupation: bending her knee into her stomach to stop the pains of hunger. Hunger has other ways of punishing her, though:

The monster had a thousand ways to torment the hungry women, never the same!... In the beginning Barbara thought that she was sick, that there was something wrong with her... It never occurred to her that all these ills came from hunger! (175)

After her mother faints from lack of food, Barbara begins to trek around Athens selling their possessions. In the middle of this private hell comes the upswing: her childhood playmate Thanasis appears, saves Barbara from her isolation, and finds her a job as well. Victoria returns, lends Barbara money, and at the same time meets her future husband, Pelopidas.

This temporary positive turn of events peaks when Thanasis and Barbara make love for the first time on the slopes of Lycabettos Hill, and in the chapter immediately following Pelopidas falls in love with Victoria. Afterwards, however, events plummet again. There ensue the series of arrests and consequent misfortunes decribed above. The novel, however, ends optimistically on the triumphant note of Greece's entry into World War II.

The duality, that is, the clear dichotomy between good and evil characters, which was seen to dominate *Boetian Earth* does not figure in *Toward a New Life*. There are few bad individuals in this world. The malevolent principal, the arresting policeman, and the police chief's dwarf are not personally responsible for the evil that befalls their victims; they are primarily agents of the Metaxas government. Barbara's mother Christina is selfish and superficial, but Barbara loves her despite her weakness, and she loves Barbara. Her coldness is attributed to her "good upbringing." Moreover, Christina recognizes the vacuity of her values as she comes to love Victoria and Thanasis, who are not of the upper class, and when she sees the corruption of the young man she wanted her daughter to marry. Embracing Barbara and Thanasis at the end, she effects a unification of generations, of class, and of spirit which is the thrust of this novel.

Point of View and Style

The third-person narrator of *Toward a New Life* occasionally briefly departs from Barbara's point of view to enter the minds of other characters: Chrysa, Christina, Victoria, Pelopidas, the admiral, and even a police officer in the courtyard of the interrogation headquarters.

The narrator takes an informal stance with regard to the reader, even at times interrupting the account to philosophize. For example, early in the novel, when Barbara is teaching at the boys' high school, a young student named Yiannos who habitually daydreams in class runs up to her and presents her with a paper butterfly he has made. The unidentified narrator asks coyly,

Now tell me, when the sensitive little schoolboy Yiannos runs to present his teacher with the butterfly he has been making instead of listening to the lesson, would it have been possible for anyone to hit Yiannos, to deliver a blow to his little cheeks? It certainly wasn't possible for Barbara to do that. (13)

At other times the narrator remarks, "We forgot to say . . ." (84), or "Let's not forget . . ." (227), or "We have spoken about . . ." (279). Infrequent as they are, these intrusions create the impression of a friendly storyteller who can characterize people with emotionally tinged and evaluative adjectives, such as calling the little boy "sensitive" or, in another case, the dwarf's voice "unpleasant" (136).

The narrative persona in some cases continues to explore the ramifications of an incident. In the case of the schoolboy, again, the narrator comments that Yiannos is a poet; he himself is like a butterfly trapped in the dismal classroom, and so is Barbara, his teacher. Adopting an omniscient point of view, the narrator reveals the boy's feelings about the butterfly he has made and then the teacher's: "The child had the illusion that he held a living butterfly in his hands. In other words, that he held in his two hands one of the beauties of the world!" The child begs his teacher not to send him to the principal for inattention, saying that he loses his senses when the principal yells at him. "The little teacher thinks that exactly the same thing happens to her... she can't bear to hear the principal shout either, not even at the children. And all of a sudden she realizes how much she resembles Yiannos... and all of a sudden she loves the child even more..." (14).

Nakos's simple demotic language, with nearly conversational constructions and poetic phrasing, is also designed to reach the *laos,* the masses whom the author believes literature must serve. She uses many diminutive endings to create a feeling of intimacy and tenderness, such as Yiannos's *magoulakia* ("little cheeks)," and *daskalitsa* ("little teacher"). This is particularly effective when contrasted with formal phrasing. For example, in the dungeon of the security police headquarters,

Here in the cellar of the Security Police they heaped the citizens, men and women of the Kingdom of Greece, whose little grandfathers once spilled their blood in '21 to free themselves from the Turkish yoke. (147)

Nakos uses the word *pappoulides* for "grandfathers." The diminutive ending on the word *pappous* yields something like "little grandpas," creating a strong sense of affection for the grandfathers who fought and died in the Revolution, and closeness between them and their grandchildren who are now suffering under "another tyranny." This then contrasts with the formal "citizens, men and women of the Kingdom of Greece," creating a cool distance from and an ironic belittling of that Kingdom. Thus through her use of the demotic language and the narrator's point of view, Nakos creates a closeness and sympathy with the reader which renders her "message" more available as well.

A Positive View of Love and Sex

In addition to its political theme, the most striking aspect of this novel is its positive view of love, and the integration of sex into that view. In earlier works Nakos portrays young girls and young women with mostly negative attitudes toward sex. In *Boetian Earth* the adolescent Barbara feels guilty about meeting Thanasis in the woods to kiss, and she chooses to spend her time instead by the bedside of Andreas, with whom she feels a purely spiritual bond. Thanasis at that time correctly accuses her of separating the soul and the body and preferring the former.

In *Toward a New Life* Andreas is back on his Swiss mountaintop, close to the sky and far from Barbara, who is now ready to accept Thanasis' earthy love. She tells him,

"Yes, Thanasis, I love Andreas, I don't hide it from you. Indeed, until the time I saw you again, I believed that I loved only him in the world. But I love him as an exceptional being. . . . But now, Thanasis, that I saw you before me... sturdy and strong... I felt that real love is not to love only the other's soul, but his body too..." (197)

It is true that Barbara is pleased that Thanasis does not approach her sexually when they meet secretly in her attic. In keeping with the social standards of the time, "It seemed to her that in this way he showed his affection more deeply" (228). But when the couple find themselves in a pine forest, close to the earth, shortly before Thanasis is to leave on a Party mission, the two are irresistibly drawn to each other; they no longer are able nor wish to suppress their physical longing for each other.

Barbara's first sexual experience is romantic and perfect, totally different from the disastrous first lovemaking in *The Lost,* when Kostas leaves Alexandra naked in bed in a deserted country inn, and their affair is effectively ended. In contrast, Thanasis is overcome with reverence for Barbara's womanhood, as he was when they were adolescents and he witnessed her first menstruation. The adult Thanasis, lying beside Barbara on the slopes of a hill, "felt suddenly a respect and awe for the womanly body." They make love:

> The young woman then put her mouth against his neck and then... he too rolled on top of her. It was like a strange force overtaking the two of them, like a whirlwind. As if there passed over them a fertile wind which shook them to the roots of their beings. (256)

Barbara feels no guilt after making love with Thanasis. Rather, she is elated at the thought that she may be bearing within her "a new life," and she and Thanasis repeat their experience when he spends his last night, before going off to war, in bed with her in her attic room. Barbara again feels happy, for, as the narrator observes from her point of view, "is there any greater happiness than to be beside the one you love on such a night?" (337). This happiness furnishes the novel's optimistic ending.

In Nakos's earlier works people choose the wrong partners, and love brings them nothing but suffering. Not so here. The saving power of love is nowhere clearer than in its effect on Pelopidas, the skinny, stingy university professor who lives shuttered in the upper flat of his house. When Pelopidas breaks his leg, Victoria rushes upstairs to help Christina lift him into his bed. Seeing the eccentric old bachelor in his dark apartment, caged by his neurotic fear of germs, Victoria quickly diagnoses his problem. She exhorts him to "Love, at least, some living thing, a canary, a dog, a flower!" (261). When he takes her advice and falls in love with Victoria herself, Pelopidas is reborn. He opens his shutters and his fists and returns to the world looking years younger, to become a partner in the first happily married couple in Nakos history.

Since the enemy in this novel is the state, both men and women are portrayed favorably. Barbara, Victoria, and Chrysa are matched by Thanasis, Pelopidas, and Marinos, Victoria's brother. Even the mother's circle of fallen aristocrats is more pitiable than execrable, and the old admiral who secretly admires Barbara is a sympathetic character. The favorable image of both women and men makes union between them possible. Although Barbara scorns the sort of marriage her mother envisions for her, seeing Victoria and Pelopidas stroll off after their wedding, she wonders, "Would she ever get to know the joy that every girl awaits from the one she loves?" (332). Such a romantic view of marriage is found in none of Nakos's earlier works. Both the mother and the nursemaid Marina in *Nafsika* curse marriage, and Alexandra in *The Lost* wants only to be near her beloved Kostas, vowing never to seek to marry him. In *Toward a New Life* even Thanasis, a dedicated Communist, believes in marriage. When Barbara is surprised to hear this, he explains,

> As long as society remains the same, you can't put the woman you love in a compromising position. No one must have the right to insult her. Marriage came about in order to protect the woman and children. And it seems to me unforgivable egoism for a man to live illegally with a woman he loves. I abhor only arranged marriages whose motive is the dowry. (222)

Thus *Toward a New Life* constitutes a new development in Nakos's portrayal of the human condition. It ends with one happy marriage and the promise of another.

Victoria, The Moustached Heroine

The most eloquent statement about women in *Toward a New Life* is the character appropriately named Victoria, the most delightful and significant of Nakos's many eccentric characters. She is an androgynous midwife, a heroine in the tradition of Jesse James, a female Zorba with a touch of Mary Poppins—an enormous, independent, strong-armed "battleship" who, decked out in a Scotch plaid skirt and a huge straw hat, and carrying a red umbrella, is ready to roll up her sleeves at any moment and administer "Swift Justice," in accordance with her nickname.

Victoria is an idealized mother/savior who comes to Barbara's aid whenever she is needed. Victoria is Barbara's polar opposite in her strength and her ability to stand up for her rights and the rights of others. If Barbara is tiny, shy, and naive, a caricature of Nakos's humble self-image, Victoria is an embodiment of the author's fantasy. Nakos herself expressed this. "I would have liked to be like Mrs. Victoria,"[4] she said when discussing this novel, and she waved her arm in mock administration of justice and uttered syllables to suggest staccato blows: "Tsak, tsuk, tsuk, tsuk. But since I was a little thing, what could I do?" So she created the character of Victoria.

Many of Nakos's earlier works contain characters who are forerunners of Victoria: large, androgynous, competent, motherly, often moustached women. The earliest such figure, in *The Lost*, is Sister Pagratia, the good-hearted nun who comes to the aid of Alexandra's family when everyone else has deserted them. In that novel, too, is another predecessor: Señora Lola, the old singer who takes care of Alexandra at the cabaret where she plays piano. But Lola herself is defeated, cast out, to be replaced by a young singer.

In *Nafsika* Mme Germaine is a large, expansive woman with a moustache who knows all about life and whom no one dares to cross. Mme Germaine has Victoria's spirit, but not her passion for justice. This passion is found in the cook in *Boetian Earth*, when she speaks up to save Piavelis at his trial. The culmination of this line of women is Victoria, who fears no one and loves justice above all.

Victoria is also the last in a line of Nakos midwives. Like the maid Asimina in *Nafsika* and the strange neighbor Argyro in *Boetian Earth*, Victoria herself is childless. In the earlier works the role of midwife entails mysterious power, but in keeping with the realistic tone of the present novel, Victoria's power is concrete: the strength of her arms and her will. It is appropriate, metaphorically, for Victoria to bring new lives into the world; she also brings new life to Pelopidas, the man she marries, and she helps usher in the new life of justice which she and her fellow characters long for.

Victoria's ability to act distinguishes her happily from her predecessors in another way. The earlier women are coupled with worthless men. Mme Germaine is still tending her husband who has given up his dissolute life only because he is paralyzed. The cook in *Boetian Earth* fails to marry the arch-villain Skoureas only because he, not she, reneged. Asimina's husband was a smuggler. Victoria, in contrast, lived with her first husband only a year. As soon as she discovered his evil nature, she booted him out, apparently wasting no tears over him. Thus Victoria is perhaps the only truly independent female character Nakos has created. She is financially self-sufficient, and she derives satisfaction from her work as well as from her administration of "Swift Justice."

Nakos invokes two sources of Greek pride, its ancient heritage and the 1821 Revolution, in characterizing this startling heroine. She characterizes Victoria as a modern Bouboulina (314), associating her with the renowned heroine of the Revolution. Victoria is also described as "a modern Demeter with a little moustache" (202), linking her with the ancient earth goddess. This association is further reinforced by Victoria's origins: she is a mountain woman, a villager, earthy and fat. Just as the mythological Demeter descends into Hades to retrieve her daughter Persephone, so Victoria descends into the underworld of the Secret Police to save Barbara after she has dipped into the first and second circles of hell, as the sections of police headquarters are called. To pursue this analogy, when Victoria takes on the sadistic dwarf, it is as if she were grappling with Cerberus, the dog at the gate of Hades, for the dwarf is called the Police Chief's "bulldog," and the "police dog," since he bites prisoners like a rabid canine.[5]

One of the triumphs of *Toward a New Life* is the character Victoria, called, variously, "a madwoman," "a virago," "vast," "huge," "a battleship," "strong-armed," and "a woman colossus."

Chrysa, A Martyred Worker

Victoria introduces Barbara to Chrysa, who shares a name as well as the circumstances of her life and death with the friend Nakos described when she discussed her reasons for writing this novel. The character Chrysa contrasts with Barbara in a number of ways. Barbara is a dreamer; Chrysa is "a tireless little ant," in the words of the novel as well as the speech Nakos attributed to the real-life Chrysa as quoted earlier. The fictionalized Chrysa is a worker in a factory and for the Communist Party. Nevertheless, as Victoria tells the two girls, "You're the same in your hearts if not in your minds, that is, your ideas" (97). Chrysa is central to the novel in two ways. Her friendship with Barbara contributes to the optimistic world view that permits bonds between people who, in Nakos's early works, were hopelessly isolated. Second, Chrysa's arrest, torture, and death provide the central, wrenching image of the theme of political oppression, injustice, and human suffering which dominates the book. Moreover, it is Chrysa's firm faith in a new life and a better world that gives the novel its title and ultimate hope. The novel contains at least thirty occurrences of such phrases as "a better life," "a better tomorrow," "the betterment of life," "a better day."

Toward a New Life does not have the aura of magic and mystery that many earlier Nakos works have, and the attraction that these characters feel for each other is earthy, not mystical. The single character who bears a spiritual aura about her is Chrysa, who emerges as a Christ figure. Her name not only suggests "Christ" but also means "gold" and describes the color of her hair: "Her hair made a contrast with her dark face. It was like gold, a little dark on her forehead and, as she stood there and the sun played in it, it created around her a small luminous halo" (95). The halo augments Chrysa's saintly image which is also created by her self-sacrifice and martyrdom. Furthermore, she is the only character in this work associated with supernatural forces. She attracts people with her expression, and her eyes have a "mysterious" quality (95). When Barbara visits her just before her arrest, there is an eery atmosphere created by the hooting of an owl, believed by peasants to be a bad omen.

Political Oppression and the Human Condition

The presence of the character Chrysa, a Communist martyr, underscores the fact that *Toward a New Life* is Nakos's most political novel. Its main impact is as a protest against the Metaxas dictatorship, and it was recognized as such, resulting in the harassment of its author. In fact, however, while it is virulently anti-fascist, the novel is not pro-Communist; despite her many

Communist friends, Nakos never endorsed Communism.[6] The view presented in this novel is similar to that in Nakos's first major work, *The Deflowered One*. The characters who are Communists are sympathetic, and the phobic attitude of the upper class toward Communists is ridiculed. However, a wise commentator within the novel points out that, although the intentions of individual Communists are benevolent, yet Communist dogma is unsound.

The absurdity of the upper-class view of Communists is shown in Christina's Thursday evening card-playing friends with their French phrases and empty chatter. "Have you ever seen a Communist?" one of Christina's friends whispers. These poverty-stricken aristocrats live in terror of the Communists stealing from the rich, even though they personally have nothing left but their high opinions of themselves.

Thanasis and Chrysa are both active Communists, and they are both heroic humanitarians. But while Barbara loves them both, Nakos makes her judgment clear in the comments of the all-knowing Victoria who says repeatedly that the division into parties will destroy Greece; that partisanship is evil because it creates hate as well as love; that the Communist Party devours its own children and abandons its members when it no longer needs them; and that Marx was a "Satan" who "has taken so many people on his neck" (95).

Communist or not, the sympathetic characters want to see "a new life" of peace and justice and economic equality. The portrait of the situation as it existed in Greece at the time is grim and is particularly tragic in contrast with the hope that engendered and followed the series of bloody revolutions against Turkish rule. "Is this why our grandfathers fought and sacrificed?" Barbara and her friends continually ask. The theme prominent in *Boetian Earth* recurs as well: there can be no freedom in poverty (124).

Ironically, while fighting for freedom from economic oppression, the Communists themselves are not free, having given themselves up to the Party. Thanasis admits this (190), and it is why Victoria angrily resists Chrysa's efforts to recruit her, preferring to remain "a captain of one" (111). Even Barbara begins to hate the Party, not only because it takes Thanasis away from her, but because of the self-denying passion with which he adores it.

On another level, the ultimate one perhaps, as in *Boetian Earth*, Greece's imprisonment is a reflection of the inescapable limitation from which all people suffer: the imprisonment of human souls within human bodies. Chrysa senses this:

> Sometimes I feel something strange, as if my soul is imprisoned in this body and struggles to escape, and because it's bursting inside this body; that's why I throw myself headfirst into my work, to forget what's tormenting me. (275)

Thus the political message, important as it is in this novel, comes hand in hand with Nakos's perennial concern with personal, spiritual struggles.

A Testament to Greekness

By its very nature as a political document, *Toward a New Life* constitutes an expression of commitment to Greece such as has been seen to dominate Occupation and post-Occupation Greek literature. This novel wails, "Wretched Greece, wretched fatherland," "Cursed country!" Barbara recalls the Sikelianos poem, "Conscience of Our Land," wondering where this conscience has gone, where it will be found. Yet she loves even the dust of Attica (23). The novel makes a statement of commitment to life and struggle in Greece that is in stark contrast with Nakos's early Europe-oriented work. This conviction is attributed to Barbara:

> She felt deeply bound to this land. She had deep roots in the earth she walked on, and the more it suffered, the more she loved it! The Greek soil wasn't like any other. It was made of the dust of our grandfathers who freed it from the Turk, it was made of the Ancient ancestors who illuminated and gave shape to matter with their spirit... It was made even of the dust of our own beloved dead... How can anyone, then, without wrenching, leave for good, uproot himself thus to distant foreign countries? Doesn't each of us have a duty to do something to better life in this unhappy land? (162)

In witing this novel, Nakos tried to do something to better life in her unhappy land.

An eloquent indictment of the Metaxas dictatorship, of all dictatorships, *Toward a New Life* is a piercing cry for freedom in Greece. In this unfortunate world, love of freedom is considered subversive. Barbara mentions repeatedly that she loves freedom above all else. She tells this to the high school principal to explain why she could not possibly be a member of a political party. To him, this is an admission of dangerous anarchism!

Dreading her impending appearance before the Security Police, Barbara comforts herself that her terrifying experience will serve her. "That way she would know better what was going on in her country and how the people were being tortured. One day, in fact, she would be able to write it, with no other purpose—not out of revenge or malice—but just so the young, who were just beginning their lives, would learn the value of freedom, and how one must never bend one's head to anyone who sits on one's back" (40).

As the day of the interrogation approaches, Barbara imagines what her grandfather would say to her if he were alive: "Inside, a person can always keep the soul free! What do you care if they take you to the Security Police? Look around you; just make sure that one day you tell what you saw, so it will never happen again ..." (74). Finally, in her exhilaration at the end, Barbara is inspired: "And then she thought that with her pen and her writing, she too might perhaps offer something to the struggle" (340). As she leaves the house, she searches frantically for her pen.

Like the stories Nakos wrote depicting the horrors of the German Occupation in Athens (*The Children's Hell*), the novel *Toward a New Life* represents her contribution to the struggle: the work of an "engaged" writer. Just as a number of characters in the stories of *The Children's Hell* expound their love for all people and their refusal to hate even their "enemies," so the present novel emerges without malice but simply as a statement of hope that the persecution of the Greek people may come to an end.

Chapter Nine
Happily Ever After:
Ikarian Dreamers

Inside Lilika Nakos's old house in Ekali, breakfast has just finished. The tiny coffee cups are empty. Nakos talks as the young women from Ikaria walk in and out. She is talking to me about their island. She says that Ikaria was her reintroduction to Greece after eight years' residence in Western Europe. A Swiss doctor had advised her to go there for the thermal springs, Nakos says, but,

When I first saw Ikaria, I didn't like it. It seemed like Hell to me after Switzerland. But the Swiss woman, my friend, said, "Wait, let's see the place." They were very good people. Right away they took care of us, they found us a room. And then, at that time, the poorest people of Greece used to go to Ikaria. And I liked that. Because . . . we used to go to the baths by motorboat, and I talked to the people, and I got to know them, because I had forgotten Greece and her troubles. And then the Ikarians were very nice people. Right away they opened their homes to me, they invited me. I made friends, with the girls and with the adults too. Ikaria isn't like the provinces because they are sea-going people, and they come back from all over the world. People that had gone to Japan, to China. And I liked that because I'm used to foreigners. Near there at the drug store in the evening many people gathered, different, interesting people. There were Jehovah's Witnesses . . . There were others from faraway places in China . . . I met someone who wanted to become a Buddhist. Real characters.

After she left Ikaria on a stretcher, Nakos never went back. But she had spent twelve summers in a row there, and the "real characters" of the island became real characters in *Oramatistes Tis Ikarias* [Ikarian Dreamers], literally, "Visionaries of Ikaria."

The Culminating Novel

Her last major novel, *Ikarian Dreamers* is strikingly different from the preceding work in numerous ways.[1] First published in 1963, it is a testament to the versatility of its author whose first novel, *The Lost,* an account of a young woman's coming of age in pre-World War I Geneva, constituted a breakthrough for the modern Greek novel in 1935. In contrast to the gloomy inner landscape that dominates Nakos's early works (*The Deflowered One, The Lost,* and *Nafsika*), *Ikarian Dreamers* is played out under the external threat of atomic war, the contemporary harbinger of total destruction. In the last chapter the sky blazes a bizarre yellow, lit up by American nuclear tests in the Mediterranean, causing earthquakes and other natural disturbances, as reported in snatches of actual newspaper accounts of the time.

In her characteristically simple language Nakos again romanticizes nature and the Greek peasant. This novel presents, moreover, the most favorable view of Greece Nakos has created. Here the drive toward expatriation is reversed. Whereas *The Deflowered One, The Lost,* and *Nafsika* concern Greeks who leave their country and move to Europe; and *Boetian Earth* and *Toward a New Life* have as protagonists Greeks who never left; *Ikarian Dreamers,* like *Mrs. Doremi,* is about former expatriates who have returned to live in their homeland. Furthermore, while Katerina in *Mrs. Doremi* finds Crete a ghastly place in many respects, and the townspeople ultimately will not accept her, in contrast, most of the Greek-Americans who return to Ikaria become happily integrated in the culture of the island.

Whereas Nakos's early works are written in the first person, and later works are written in the third person but still reflect a first-person point of view, the perspective of this last novel is not limited to that of a single character but shifts to reflect the points of view of a number of different characters in turn. The most striking aspect of *Ikarian Dreamers* is that its main protagonist is a man rather than a woman. This factor has a perceptible influence on the view of women that emerges in the work, as will be seen in the discussion which follows.

Finally, the heroes and heroines of *Ikarian Dreamers* are mature men and women in their forties and fifties, far different from the confused children and innocent young women in Nakos's earlier works. While Nakos treats sex explicitly in all her work, the main characters in the early novels and stories are not apparently driven by sexual impulses. Quite the contrary, the young women in the early fiction are intent on avoiding sexual involvement. In this last novel sex is a powerful, everpresent force rather than an undercurrent, and it directly motivates the primary characters.

Ikarian Dreamers is an intensely romantic novel, as are all Nakos's works, but it is set in the perspective of a highly sophisticated modern world.

The Story

Ikarian Dreamers begins and ends with Kosmas, a fifty-year-old New York restaurant owner, who has returned to his native Greek island to help its inhabitants by contracting with an American company to develop the island's natural radioactive springs. Kosmas is frustrated and infuriated to find the people of the island determined to resist his efforts, until he begins to understand their indifference to the money the project would yield, and their concern instead that the springs remain accessible to Greece's poor. The native Ikarians feel that if the springs are to be developed at all, they'd rather do it themselves.

Kosmas decides to abandon his plans and return to America. This is what his second wife Sophie has wanted all along (Kosmas's first wife died years before, when their two sons were very young). Sophie is also a native of Ikaria, but she never comes to understand the people she has ceased to identify with. Sophie is literally maddened by the Greek island which has cut her off from everything she now values and surrounded her with memories of a childhood she wants to forget.

Kosmas decides to make a visit to Raches, the mountain village of his birth, before returning to the United States. There he meets a saintly village woman named Despinio with whom he establishes an immediate intense physical and spiritual connection. The relationship between Kosmas and Despinio begins where Barbara's and Thanasis' relationship culminates: making love in a pine forest.

While Kosmas lingers in the village of Raches with Despinio, his wife Sophie remains in town, devoured by unrequited passion for Pandelis, a fisherman who is the leader of the resistance against Kosmas's project. Pandelis is the same man who rejected Sophie when she was a young girl in Ikaria, and he refuses her advances again. In her fury at being spurned a second time, Sophie determines to murder Pandelis' baby daughter and sets about her plan with crazed determination, abandoning it only at the very last moment when the child spontaneously embraces her. Sophie flees from the island and from her husband, who has tarried in his mountain village, and returns to her throne at the cash register in their New York restaurant.

Before Sophie leaves Ikaria, another Ikarian-American arrives. Yiannis Patsouris is a lonely hypochondriac from Chicago who has "played hide and seek" with death all his life. When Sophie leaves the island, her servant, a village girl named Paraskevi, goes to work for Patsouris, who eventually adopts her. Patsouris' reunion with Ikaria is consummated when he determines to give all his money to build a pier for the island that has finally given him peace of mind. On his way back from one final trip to the States to settle his financial affairs, Patsouris' lifetime dread is realized: he dies suddenly, alone, in a strange hotel in Paris.

As Kosmas is busy building a house in Raches for himself and Despinio, there arrives on the island an archeologist from the Dodecanese islands, Babis Mostratos, a character reminiscent of the archeologist Piavelis in *Boetian Earth*. But whereas Piavelis is an idealized, humorless figure in keeping with the tone of the earlier novel, Mostratos is an obstinate, idiosyncratic character who, together with his temperamental Greek-American niece,[2] offers comic relief at the same time that he fills everyone in on the appropriate background of ancient myth and lore. Before the novel ends, Mostratos discovers the tomb of Dionysus on the island.

Kosmas's two sons visit him in Ikaria, and both fall in love with the archeologist's niece. The younger son James is painfully disappointed when the young woman marries his older brother Stathis, but he recovers from this loss and is inspired by the Greek island to give up his aimless wandering and return to the United States to fulfill his dream of becoming an astronaut. However, Mostratos is furious about his niece's marriage and is inconsolable when she returns with her new husband to America, where he has taken over Kosmas's profitable businesses. Mostratos's intransigence causes a rift between him and Kosmas, but when his friend comes to tell him that they have a grandchild, Mostratos relents and the two men resume their friendship.

Kosmas and Despinio marry and move into their home, but their happiness is marred by the precariousness of the world situation. Despinio has a vision of atomic annihilation, followed by an actual terrifying test explosion of an American nuclear bomb, with bizarre aftereffects. Despinio announces that she is pregnant, and the couple consider an abortion because of the state of the world, but they reject that alternative and reaffirm their faith in a better future.

The Point of View Broadens

At the beginning of *Ikarian Dreamers* the narrator sounds strikingly like Nakos herself talking, for example, about the characters who will figure in the novel: "I happened to know them myself when I used to live near them summers in Ikaria."[3] Similarly, in these early pages, an insight is justified by the explanation, "Kosmas once revealed to me. . . ." This narrative stance soon disappears, however, dissolving into omniscience. There remains only an occasional journalistic intrusion like "as we have said above" (147), or, of the people in a crowd, "How can we enumerate all of them now?" (191).

With these few exceptions, the narrative voice which takes over after the introductory section is omniscient: one who is with Kosmas and Despinio in the woods, and on the road to Denver with Kosmas's son James. Although omniscient, however, the narrator is not objective. For example, in Raches, Kosmas stays at a small hotel owned by a local man who lived many years in Jamaica, West Indies, and is therefore called "the Jamaican."

Happily Ever After: Ikarian Dreamers

When the Jamaican doubts Despinio's tales of having seen ancient spirits, he is said to be "repeating, like a parrot, the words of the teacher" whom he quotes as calling the Greeks "unenlightened" (55). This is reminiscent of a similar technique used in *Boetian Earth,* when those who doubt the powers of Sister Timothea are characterized as narrow-minded and half-educated.

Repetition is used effectively, like a refrain, to convey a sense of the mysterious forces driving Kosmas and Sophie. Sophie, again and again, is said to have a little snake biting at her heart, while Kosmas's heart is repeatedly called a broken watch. The consciousness of the narrator dovetails with that of the character when Kosmas himself thinks of his heart as a broken watch (199). On another occasion, a narrative begun by Kosmas's son James about the arrival of the archeologist in Raches dissolves, cinematically, into the accustomed omniscient narrator's point of view.

In general, the use of this flexible narrative voice and changing perspectives is successful in portraying a wide range of characters in psychological depth that is not seen in earlier Nakos works and clearly represents a development in her style.

A Collective Consciousness

The threat of atomic war is felt throughout *Ikarian Dreamers* and threatens the personal happiness of the characters who are otherwise well suited to each other. As in all Nakos's works, the characters' psychological development cannot proceed separately from the situation of the world around them. The link between the personal and political, moreover, works both ways, and this contributes to an overriding theme in *Ikarian Dreamers* which represents another indication of the development of Nakos's style over time. In her earlier works people are seen as helpless victims of the social and political systems under which they live. In the present novel people realize that they are responsible for the world they live in. As the indifferent voice of a radio announcer drones in the background telling of the atomic bomb tests, Kosmas and Despinio ask each other, ask themselves,

Whose fault is it? until Kosmas answers, angrily, "I'll tell you whose fault it is! It's our fault! It's my fault, it's your fault, it's everybody's fault! It's the fault of the herd of people who don't speak up, who don't stand up, who leave their fate in the hands of those who govern the world, surrounded, for advisors, by careless and greedy people who don't see what destruction they're leading us toward." (245)

This message of collective responsibility is combined with a refusal to blame others which is prominent in *The Children's Hell* too. In *Ikarian Dreamers,* this attitude is again taken toward World War II.

Everyone on the island lost relatives in the Second World War. Despinio's husband and brother were killed, and her father was blinded. Kosmas wonders why the old man is not bitter about having been so badly wounded when he wasn't guilty of anything. Despinio's father explains,

"Indeed I was guilty. For I'm also a piece, you might say, a hand of the body of the people. And when people are slaughtered, whether I or someone else suffers, it's the same thing. I feel that all people are the same. So if we're all the same, we're all guilty for whatever evil occurs in the world." (170)

The notion of collective guilt is at the core of the novel and of Nakos's thought, part of the idea that all people are connected to each other and to the land they were born in.

Another interesting aspect of *Ikarian Dreamers* is that, instead of reflecting Greek political issues, it is concerned with international politics. Whereas Nakos's early work is Europe-oriented, and her later books focus on Greece alone, the Greece of 1962 described in this novel is firmly planted in the modern world, smack in the middle of the Cold War. It is Nakos's only work that deals with the United States, and it shows a surprising grasp of American issues and customs, considering that Nakos has never been there and speaks no English at all. At one point in the novel Kosmas makes a trip to the American Embassy in Athens, where he discusses John Kennedy's candidacy for the presidency.

At the same time, the Ikarians are fascinated by the Russian space flight and fall in with the fashion by renaming their fishing boats "Sputnik." Communism is a force to be reckoned with, in this as in other Nakos novels. Kosmas has to make the trip to the American Embassy because some villainous types who want to discredit him spread rumors that he is a Communist. While there, he discusses the McCarthy era with an embassy official.

As in other Nakos novels, the Communists are neither lionized nor deplored. Patsouris, the Greek-American from Chicago, realizes for the first time that "Communists are human like everybody else, and not monsters, as they were made out to be" (132). Although no characters in the novel are identified as Communists, yet there are men like the fisherman Pandelis who believes that a world will come where there will no longer be rich and poor, and it comforts him to think that there are many others who believe this too (71).

Patsouris learns about Greece's problems from his friend, a fisherman named Diamandis:

He learned of the unemployment that devastated the country. He learned that there were still political prisoners in exile on the islands, fifteen years after the civil war. He learned that the young people were leaving as emigrants to Australia, or the factories of Germany. And that the houses in the villages were being deserted. (131)

These problems, however, are cataloged by Diamandis, not portrayed in the novel, nor is the struggle of poor workers dramatized. Rather, the workers are seen in this book as idealized heroes who actually prefer their poverty.

The novel contains general references to the culpability of the government in failing to develop the Ikarian hot springs for the benefit of the inhabitants. "But this is another story," says the narrator, journalistically, "and it is not our concern to tell the story of the competition for the hot springs of Greece" (9). The novel, then, only suggests the problems that bedevil Greece, while it concentrates its energy on the vivid portrayal of international problems and tensions.

The Power of the Greek Land

The island of Ikaria represents a link between the returning Greek-Americans and their heritage and true nature. It has a vital power that affects all its inhabitants; the native Ikarians are all "dreamstruck" *(oneiroparmeni)* and, as in the title, "visionaries" *(oramatistes)*. If the Greek-Americans can yield to the island's forces, they are saved. If they cannot or will not submit, they are condemned to the corrupt and dismal life associated with American capitalism.

Ikaria's history is multiply significant. A major and recurrent theme is the connection between Ikarians of today and the mythical hero from whom the island takes its name: Icarus, son of Daedalus, the great artisan who fashioned wings so that he and his son could fly out of the labyrinth in which they were imprisoned. The overzealous boy flew too close to the sun, the wax in his wings melted, and he fell to his death in the sea. Icarus's impulse to fly too high may be reflected in the modern Ikarians' devotion to their freedom and independence.

The island is not only the site of Icarus's tomb, as the archeologist Mostratos explains; it is also the birthplace of another ancient figure, the god Dionysus, God of Wine, who is associated with revelry and sexual abandon. Hence the island's strong sexual force which suffuses the novel and motivates the characters.

On still another level, ancient lore becomes fused with the Christian tradition, as has been seen in earlier works (most prominently, *The Deflowered One*). Mostratos again supplies the information: the earliest Christians found refuge in Ikarian woods, and the island is the site of the oldest church in the western world. It is often repeated throughout the novel that both Christian saints and ancient gods live on in Ikaria, and the Ikarians, visionaries that they are, see both. When Despinio reports having seen God walking among the ancient columns of classical ruins,

"Which God?" Kosmas asked, surprised.
"The ancient God, of course. Do you think I'm the only one who's seen him? The villagers know that the ancient Gods roam our land on clear nights... Everyone knows the statues are haunted... Don't you

believe that here on our island these Gods never died; they just became spirits." (54)

When Kosmas himself is enough in tune with the island to sense these spirits, he is comforted by them. In Raches, his village,

> Kosmas lived without feeling the loneliness that used to torment him, in this faraway corner of Ikaria, in an old world, warmed by the breath of people that passed over this island thousands of years before. A world that left its tracks behind it, warmed by old tales of gods that hadn't entirely died. Pan lived on, as a satyr, and his companions changed their names and became *kallikantzaroi*.[4] They lived in the deep caves by the cape or under the ruined temple. And on moonlit nights in January, many were the villagers who saw them roaming the deserted land. (88)

Ikaria is a mystical, enchanted setting resembling idealized "otherworlds" seen in earlier Nakos fiction: close to nature, peopled by Greek peasants. For the first time, however, this paradisiacal setting is neither a brief and unreal memory nor a temporary escape. It is the real world of the island and of the novel, and the characters can remain in its protective surroundings if they so choose.

The geographical location of this island lends itself to yet another theme as well. Situated between mainland Greece and Asia Minor, Ikaria lies next to the island of Samos, which hugs the Turkish coast. Thus the Asia Minor disaster, which raised the issue of Greekness for all Greeks, is felt especially keenly in Ikaria. When Kosmas is on his way to his village, and by implication his own roots, he becomes aware of this proximity. He is riding with other travelers in a hired car:

> Way over there could be seen the mountains of Asia Minor and Samos next to them. A traveler waved his hand in that direction . . . , "Over there is Cesme. Holy soil, blessed land... We had our fields there," he said and sighed with grief. It was apparent that he was from Asia Minor. The other travelers, who weren't refugees, but natives, also sighed. Before the Catastrophe Ikarians and Samiotes went and worked

in Smyrna. They were all still leaning psychologically toward Asia Minor. It was a second homeland to them.[5] (37)

Seeing the grief of the Asia Minor refugee, Kosmas realizes that separation from the homeland is like what "a baby must feel when it is pulled from its mother's breast" (87). It is the deprivation that he himself was suffering, albeit unconsciously, when he lived in the United States, far from his Greek homeland.

For those who are able to return to their homeland, Ikaria's spell is healing. At the start of the novel, Kosmas is a nervous, ill man who must take one pill to sleep and another to eat. His heart thumps in his chest "like a broken watch." As soon as he goes to Raches, however, he sleeps perfectly and is never again troubled by his heart.

Yiannis Patsouris looks twenty years older than his age when he first comes to Ikaria, but when Kosmas comes back from Raches and finds his old friend sitting on his balcony in town, free at last from the loneliness that tailed him all his life, he hardly recognizes Patsouris who is looking years younger. Similarly, Kosmas's younger son James is in anguish when he first visits his father on the island. James has only three loves: listening to jazz in Denver, spending time with his older friend Eddy, and running away. But none of these activities ever satisfied him. When Kosmas's older son Stathis comes to Ikaria, he finds his brother James "transformed," awakened to the beauties of nature and to the physical and emotional intensity of love for the archeologist's niece. "From a yellowed weakling that he had been, he had become a ruddy-cheeked and sturdy young man" (172).

James doesn't stay in Ikaria for good; neither does his brother Stathis. They are Americans, and they return to their own homeland. But Ikaria is their heritage, and it gives them direction. Stathis marries the archeologist's niece, and James becomes a modern-day Icarus who will fly high, not with wax wings but in an American rocket. James returns to America and becomes an astronaut. The narrator of *Ikarian Dreamers* looks into the future to predict this information which supplies a symbolic and romantic conclusion in keeping with the modernistic outlook of this last novel.

A Destructive Force

Ikaria transforms everyone. Just as Kosmas hardly recognizes his friend Patsouris, so Patsouris, when he arrives, does not recognize Kosmas's wife Sophie. But Sophie has changed for the worse. Since she cannot embrace Ikaria, she is nearly destroyed by its power. Patsouris finds that "her pleasant and cheerful face, which he had liked so much before, was now morose" (77). Sophie herself feels, "As soon as she set foot on this cursed island, everything changed inside her. She didn't recognize herself any more. What could have happened to her? She still couldn't figure out the secret of her soul" (122).

Sophie is out of control, driven mad by a "little snake" inside her heart, a devil that has taken possession of her, driving her to murder Pandelis' little girl because he spurned her advances. Although she stops short of committing this crime, Sophie does not conquer the devil in her heart. Rather, she gives herself up to it, by returning to New York and devoting herself to the accumulation of wealth with the same blind monomania with which she had pursued Pandelis in Ikaria. Sophie's destructive sexual energy is the antithesis of Kosmas's fruitful passion for Despinio. Neither understands the source of these obsessions. Ikaria has a secret power that is closely connected to the forces of nature.

Ikaria's intimate connection with nature is in stark contrast with the modern rejection of nature as epitomized by life in New York, where Kosmas and Sophie were entombed in a restaurant under a monstrous skyscraper. Sophie hadn't looked at the sky in twenty years. Both Kosmas and Sophie are reminded in Ikaria that they were happy as children in their poor villages, where they were barefoot but close to nature. Kosmas rediscovers in Raches "a joy that had totally abandoned him from the time he had shepherded goats on this land, even if he had been barefoot then and eaten dry bread and olives" (43). Sophie has a similar flash of insight:

She was taken back by the memory of that little girl, barefoot, orphaned, who pastured the village sheep for a plate of soup. . . . But that little girl, Sophie remembered well, had joy in her heart then, when she went out into the country! She sang, she jumped, she was happy. The sun, the sea, the air, the first rains, filled her with joy. There was a time, when, bent face down, she enjoyed looking at the little ants and the earth; as she bent, smelling thyme, she remembered. And, suddenly, she felt what "fatherland" means! (23)

However, Sophie chooses to turn her back on the child that she was, as she scolds and insults Paraskevi, the village orphan who works for her, and as she longs to return to her restaurant tomb.

Until she makes her decision in favor of New York and against Ikaria, a battle rages in Sophie: "Inside her two women struggled, the good and the bad" (120). In this sense the narrator of the novel is somewhat heavy-handed. The romantic notion of childhood happiness is associated with Sophie's "good" impulses, her true self, while the drive to reject that is "bad."

In keeping with this split, all the Greek-Americans have two names: their "true" Greek names, and the false names they are called in America. Sophie is really "Sofia," but since she embraces American values, she is always called "Sophie." Kosmas has not changed his first name, but his surname, Baxibanopoulos, has been truncated to "Box," reflecting metaphorically the fact that his true nature was limited in America just as the syllables of his name were lopped off. Since Kosmas chooses in favor of the "good" voice inside himself and gives up to Ikaria's charms, he feels "as if he had found his old self again" (42).

The specter of what might have become of Kosmas if he had not abandoned his materialistic values is embodied in the character bearing the nickname "Mr. Dollars." Once the richest Greek-American in New York, Mr. Dollars is now a lunatic lottery vender in the villages of Ikaria. Dragging from his pockets crumpled photographs of himself with important Americans, he speaks in choppy sentences with a ridiculous American accent: "Here, Mr. Dollars gives speech, consortium, big dinner! Here, conference, Mr. Dollars president!" To underscore his alienation from his true nature, the total loss of his Ikarian identity, "He spoke about himself as if he were speaking about someone else—about a third person" (197). Mr. Dollars is still dedicated to the

Happily Ever After: Ikarian Dreamers

cultivation of wealth, in the absurd form of a dollar tree which he waters daily, believing the old paper money he has stuck onto its branches will grow into real dollars. Throughout the novel a love of money symbolizes corrupt values. It is this passion that lures Sophie back to her restaurant, where she sits in perennial darkness, ringing up dollars in her cash register. In contrast, native Ikarians scorn money. Patsouris' friend, the fisherman Diamandis, refuses to accept money to have his house fixed; he prefers the pleasure of gradual saving, planning the repairs bit by bit, and enjoying with his wife the slow improvement of their home. Kosmas's village lover, Despinio, scorns money most of all. She is outraged when Kosmas offers her a diamond ring after their first encounter in the pine forest. She later confesses to the other village women that Kosmas "has one failing: they say he has a lot of money" (168). When he too learns not to revere wealth, Kosmas is redeemed.

The Power of Sexual Love

Ikaria's healing power is related to the healing power of love. Although Kosmas never argues with Sophie, neither does he feel anything for her. Both have been too busy making money to notice each other. When he sees the great need that Mostratos the archeologist has for his niece, Kosmas realizes, "Old or young, no one can live isolated, without affection, without love!" (223). This is a message that is conveyed in other works by Nakos, especially in *Toward a New Life*. However, for the first time, love in this novel is deeply sexual.

As Sophie senses, "Sex reigned everywhere" on this island, the birthplace of Dionysus. Sophie is obsessed with her desire for Pandelis:

> She wanted him for herself, to sleep with him. The longing of her body increased day by day and muddied her mind. Who knows? Perhaps it was the fault of the climate which had changed, perhaps that she had no work to do, perhaps her forty years which boiled her blood and made her feel the last flame of youth. (35–36)

The omnipresent sexual force is destructive in Sophie because for her it is not fused with love. She has never loved anyone (32). Sophie is nearly saved by the magic power of the love shown her by Pandelis' little girl. After throwing her arms impetuously around Sophie's neck, the child grabs a gold locket Sophie wears on a gold chain, a significantly "empty heart." When Sophie tries to leave, having thrown away the poisoned milk she had been about to feed the child, the little girl continues to clutch the locket. Sophie gives it to her, announcing, "It was empty. It was worthless because it was empty. Now this little heart is filled, and it's yours!" (117) However, after she recovers from a feverish swoon which lasts for an undetermined period, a swoon such as Nakos characters often undergo following traumatic experiences, Sophie's spiritual struggle is won by the "bad" part of her which cannot love.

While Ikaria's sexual power becomes destructive in Sophie, it is a positive force for Kosmas, as well as for other characters. Kosmas meets Despinio when he thinks he is alone in a pine forest and has been overcome with a sudden and unaccountable hunger. Despinio appears like a vision and gives him a piece of fresh-baked village bread.[6] Kosmas feels himself drawn irresistibly to her:

And suddenly there was a surge inside him; an unconquerable longing for the woman's body overcame him. Without realizing what he was doing, he lay down on the earth next to her. . . . He squeezed her to him with passion. For a few seconds he lost the awareness of a sense of time. Caught, both of them, in the net of a force all mystery, they had their bodies unite in a fleshly throb which intoxicated them. (47)

This intense and sudden physical passion seems natural: "The attraction of their bodies didn't surprise them," for these are fully mature adults. Furthermore, the sexual bond is a sign of the deep spiritual rapport between the two, which is consummated in marriage and becomes fruitful.

Complex Characterizations

Despite the clearly romantic nature of the novel's portrayal of love and other forces, the characters in *Ikarian Dreamers* are not two-dimensional, like those in Nakos's early work, but rather are fully developed and psychologically complex, a pattern which is made possible by the narrator's omniscient point of view.

Characters in this novel are not clearly distinguished as "good" and "bad." Sophie, though ultimately representing the wrong values, is not without redeeming qualities, and the inner struggle she experiences is recounted with sympathy. Moreover, she undergoes her agonizing ordeal quite alone, while no one suspects her turmoil. Kosmas, by the same token, is not a blameless hero. He is unmistakably egotistical, never having noticed his wife in all the years of their marriage (12).

Kosmas shows no hint of concern that Sophie never wanted to make the trip to Ikaria, nor that she is suffering there. He leaves her alone in town and goes off to Raches, where he happily consorts with Despinio, totally forgetting his wife. Yet he is furious when he returns to town much later and discovers that she has left him to return to America. Even though she tells him in a farewell note that she has passed through a great crisis, he thinks only of the insult to himself. He self-pityingly recalls his first wife: "She would never have done such a thing, to get up and go, and leave me" (139). He sulks to Despinio: "Just think, I found the house closed up and myself all alone! Can you imagine how it struck me at that moment to learn from the neighbors that my wife left... Is such a thing possible? Did you ever hear of such an insult!" (145). Kosmas feels no sense of responsibility or guilt about not having been in touch with his wife for so long, since he became involved with Despinio. His concern with "insult" is the sort of superficiality Nakos always exposes in the upper middle class. It takes Kosmas hardly more than a day to forget both the insult and the wife who perpetrated it.

Yiannis Patsouris, the third protagonist, walks a middle ground between Kosmas and Sophie. In the beginning he is isolated like Sophie in a world without love, agonized by his terror of dying alone. Like Kosmas, however, he is redeemed by

Ikaria. Yet Patsouris leaves the island, albeit unwillingly, to make a last trip to the United States, and he dies alone before he can return to it. Patsouris' fate underscores a theme that recurs in all Nakos's work, although it is less prominent in this than in others: "A person lives all alone, a stranger to the person beside him, and great is his loneliness" (128).

Kosmas, Sophie, and Yiannis Patsouris are complex figures. Only Despinio is more a symbol than a real character. When she appears to Kosmas in the woods, the sun on her blond hair makes her head shine (46), and Kosmas feels that their meeting is "holy" (50). Despinio is called "clairvoyant," "a fairy-tale teller," "dreamstruck," "spiritstruck," "a visionary." She has "her own secret rhythm" (84), and she is "lost in her own world" (173). The other village women go to her to have their dreams interpreted. When Kosmas returns to Raches after a trip to town, he tells her he has returned "for you and, if you like, for the pine forest" (145), the place where they meet to make love and where she roams "like a spirit." Despinio is "a piece of the Ikarian earth," in touch with its elements, a modern earth goddess.

Since Despinio is not a real character but in some way the symbol of Ikaria, it seems inappropriate to regard her as an indication of the development of Nakos's attitude toward women. Despinio is illiterate, and her main dream is to have a baby, for she believes, "A woman without a child is a tree without fruit, a black and joyless life for a true woman" (108). She also longs for a man, recalling her "deceased husband, the feeling of shelter and protection which she had felt beside him" (107). Kosmas speaks to Despinio "as if to a child," for "she was a simple creature, a big dreamstruck child, this Despinio" (147). Clearly, in the spirit of this work, Despinio's childlike quality is intended to denote not inferiority but great innocence and purity, in striking contrast to the corruption of the modern world. To be "dreamstruck" is not a matter of idle fantasy, but a connection to the true center of life, and to the ancient and religious spirits that make Ikaria sacred.

Nonetheless, the characterization of Sophie also seems to make this novel Nakos's least feminist work. An admirably self-sufficient woman, Sophie emerges as a negatively portrayed character, to say the least. The importance of education and a career for a woman, which is central to the novella *Nafsika* and the novel *Boetian Earth* as well as implicit in almost all Nakos's other fiction, is not supported in this last novel. Yiannis Patsouris thinks at one time of educating his adopted daughter Paraskevi, but he simply marries her off instead, and she seems quite satisfied with that arrangement.

Paraskevi's marriage is one of the celebrated triumphs of the novel, for her groom is a particularly "good catch": a handsome and sensitive young diver who is himself "dreamstruck" as he believes in mermaids and other spirits living in the sea. Yet he treats his young wife with scorn. When Paraskevi asks James, who is planning to become an astronaut, what will happen if he finds the souls of the dead in the sky, her husband snaps, "Don't talk nonsense." Then he turns to address James: "Look what women come up with if you discuss serious things in front of them" (214).

This condescending attitude toward women is the prevailing one, rather than Kosmas's exceptional respect for Despinio, and it is seen again and again in the attitude of the Ikarian men. In the exalted village of Raches the owner of the hotel where Kosmas stays has a typical view: "Women were women, in other words, inferior beings" (51). When the local men talk to their wives, they habitually address them generically as "Woman!" Even the fisherman Pandelis, who becomes a hero of sorts since he spearheads the town's refusal to sell the springs to American investors, and he resists the temptation to be unfaithful to his wife with Sophie, nevertheless talks to his wife as if she were a stupid beast. When the poor woman expresses the hope that Sophie, who has been hovering about the family, might take a protective interest in their children and pay for their son's education and their daughter's dowry, Pandelis laces into her: "Oh, you poor woman! You don't understand the times we live in. . . . What can I tell you, woman, since you don't understand?" (70). When she mentions her husband's best friend who has died, he snaps, "Drop him, woman, from your lips!" (70). These interchanges occur not in the course of arguments, but simply as part of ordinary conversations.

Commentary on the position of women, however, is indirect, not the direct focus of the novel, which is after all the story of a man, Kosmas. *Ikarian Dreamers* is a combination of such subtle documentation of the way things are, plus the symbolic representation of forces in the real world by characters such as Despinio.

As Nakos's last major novel, *Ikarian Dreamers* is a continuation of the working out of themes investigated in the author's earlier work as well as a culmination of her style in her most mature and complex novel.

Chapter Ten
Conclusion

One of the first women to write novels in Greek, Lilika Nakos has made a giant contribution to the development of the "social novel" in Greek. Her work was pioneering in two major ways: First, her use of simple demotic language furthered the cause of demoticism, that is, the acceptance and development of the spoken idiom as a literary language. Second, Nakos's novels focused on the psychological development of women as protagonists. She wrote with startling frankness about the experiences of women at every stage in their lives.[1]

Nakos's approach to literature is pragmatic; she believes that it should enlighten and give hope to its readers. Thus her novels can be seen as social documents, exposing the hardships of working people, of exploited children, and of women. Moreover, certain of her works were written with specific social purposes. Her collection of stories, *The Children's Hell*, alerted the world to the great famine in Athens during the German Occupation of World War II, and *Toward a New Life* exposes the abuses of the Metaxas dictatorship in Greece which immediately predated that war. Yet all her novels, while accurately portraying difficult, even wretched, social conditions, end on optimistic notes and reaffirm hope that things will get better.

Nakos's novels are romantic. The characters, especially in the earlier works, are monolithically good or bad. Nakos is particularly adept at portraying extreme swings of emotion so that sudden events hurl characters into exhilaration or despair. She has developed an accustomed structure that lends itself to this pattern, whereby the protagonist experiences two psychological low points, one in the middle of the book, and one just before the end, but from both of which she is precipitously saved.

If Nakos's works are grouped, they fall out something like this: The early work includes the short stories written in French and, in some cases, later rewritten in Greek; the novella *The Deflowered One* (originally published in French in 1928); Nakos's first full-length novel *The Lost* (1935); and the short stories written in Greek at about the same time as *The Lost*. In these works the protagonists are little girls or young women, innocent helpless victims in bleak environments, perpetually alone, and love is nothing but a source of torment.

The World War II period includes the stories of *The Children's Hell* and the novels *Boetian Earth* and *Toward a New Life*, in sequence. Here the focus is on renewed commitment to Greece and interest in its heritage. Although the heroine of the two novels is a young woman not unlike the earlier heroines, she is able to make somewhat satisfying connections to other people, and she feels a pride in Greece in addition to the anger sparked by the way Greece makes her people suffer.

The two works that Nakos wrote in French after she moved to Switzerland in 1947, and later rewrote in Greek, are anomalous in a number of ways. The slim, lyrical novella *Nafsika* is much more like the works of the early period than those written later. Its heroine is an unhappy, alienated little girl living with her gentle but miserable mother in Marseilles. The tone of this work, like the early works, is an agonized wail at the injustice in the world and consequent human suffering. Its message is "Never love a man." *Mrs. Doremi* is as different in tone as can be; it is Nakos's only comic novel, based on her year teaching at a boys' high school in Rethymnon, Crete.

Nakos's last novel was written in Greek after she returned once more to her homeland. *Ikarian Dreamers* (1963) evidences much development when compared to the early works. The point of view has opened out; the characters have matured (now they are middle aged men and women); and this is Nakos's only novel with a male protagonist. The themes of personal isolation and social injustice are still prominent, but for the first time the novel ends with its main characters getting married, despite the disturbing threat of atomic war.

Conclusion 165

This final marriage is particularly significant, in contrast to the attitude toward marriage in earlier works, and in *Nafsika*, where it is seen as slavery for women, when it is possible at all. Earlier works (and again *Nafsika*), and even *Boetian Earth*, stress that a woman must be educated and have an independent means of self-support; in the last novel, this insistence is not heard. Perhaps the fact that *Ikarian Dreamers* has a male protagonist alters the vision in a basic way. The novel clearly shows how men condescend to women even if it does not explicitly comment on that fact.

The development of the theme of sexual awareness in Nakos's work follows a pattern of coming of age. In the early stories the heroines are little girls who are traumatized and repelled by sex. Alexandra, whose childhood and young womanhood furnish the material for *The Lost*, is thoroughly asexual. As Barbara is seen through adolescence in *Boetian Earth*, she begins to have a positive rather than negative initiation into sexuality, but she remains ambivalent and guilt-ridden as the novel ends with her having opted for a purely spiritual bond rather than a fleshly one. In *Toward a New Life* the same heroine, Barbara, moves tentatively toward sexual union with her earthy childhood lover, but their physical relationship comes at the very end, just before the couple must separate because of the war. A true acceptance of sexuality comes in Nakos's last novel, *Ikarian Dreamers*, in the form of a fully sexual union between the repatriated Greek-American Kosmas and his Ikarian dreamer, Despinio.

Lilika Nakos was able to make a significant contribution to Greek literature because of the special circumstances of her life and character. Since she grew up in Geneva, she received a fine literary education, despite her father's objections (he lived mainly in Greece). Her Swiss education also saved her from ever having to learn *katharevousa*, the stilted language that was imposed on Greeks from their high school education on. Yet Nakos had been born in Greece; her formative years had been spent there; and she went back often to visit her father, until she returned to stay in 1930. Although she left Greece again after World War II, she ultimately returned again and retired there.

In a sense, then, Nakos's upper-class background permitted her to become educated and to have a mother with a passion for reading that she passed on to her daughter. Yet Nakos's mother did not have much money, first because her father did not want to hand it over, and then because he lost what he had and died soon after. As a result, Nakos had to work from an early age, as a pianist, a teacher, and a journalist. Thus she gained the experience of working conditions that furnished the material for her social criticism.

Of course, no constellation of events and circumstances makes a writer. Nakos was able to take advantage of her situation, she chose to take advantage of it, because of her own artistic temperament. And it was no doubt her ingenuous character, the same apparent indifference to personal consequences that makes her personally so open and irreverent, that made it possible for her to disregard her father's outrage and the leering alacrity with which Greek critics took her work as pure autobiography, and to continue to write because, as she says, she liked it.

Nakos's disarming cavalier attitude is sometimes frustrating for an exacting reader. When *The Deflowered One* was published in Greece in 1932, the critic C. Dimaras wrote an effusively laudatory review.[2] But first he enumerated the novella's weaknesses: "linguistic errors, awkwardness, countless typographical and even spelling errors; inaccuracies, chronological inconsistencies, unheard-of carelessness (the same characters change names suddenly in the middle of the body of the work), etc. Rarely have I seen a more untidy, a more uncombed, a more careless book." Finally, however, Dimaras calls the book, "An uncombed, spoiled child... but how spirited, how sweet, how lovable. The weaknesses I listed above would be enough to diminish or to kill the good impression of any other work: but here is another surprise: how strongly it draws us in and binds us, how it charms us."

Although the carelessness Dimaras describes is most evident in this first work, it is found, to some extent, in all Nakos's books. The author herself is not bothered by this fact; it seems trivial to her. She turned down my offer to help her eliminate inconsistencies in a forthcoming reprint of *Toward a New Life*,

Conclusion 167

dismissing the matter with a wave of her hand: "Oh, I haven't got the patience for that!" And so her works remain, rather like her home, even a bit like herself, at times unkempt, but always spirited and full of commitment and charm: the qualities that permitted her to portray with frankness young girls' private agonies coming of age in an often grim world, startling Greek literature into its own adolescence at the same time.

Notes and References

Chronology

1. The situation surrounding the establishment of Nakos's date of birth (a simple matter, one might have thought) is typical of the difficulty I encountered establishing chronology. Published sources cite her birth date variously as 1902, 1903, or 1905. Nakos told me that she was born in 1902, but some of her contemporaries suggested to me that she was born earlier than that. Persistent and creative sleuthing led to the discovery that the Journalists' Union lists her birth date as 1900, and the civil records list it as 1899. Nakos, however, told me that the records erroneously reflect the birth date of a baby born to her parents three years earlier than she, for whom she was named since the baby died. The birth date I have given in the chronology, then, is my best guess in the face of this confusion.

Chapter One

1. Right at the start, the critic has a problem when referring in English to a Greek woman. In Greek a woman's last name is rendered in the genitive. My subject is named LILIKA NAKOY (pronounced NAH-KOO), while her father's surname is NAKOS. Literally, she is the Lilika who belongs to Nakos. Women's names are generally translated into English in the same form as the husband's or father's name. Thus, I have elected to use NAKOS. Furthermore, this is the name under which Nakos's early stories were translated and published in the United States. Her publications in France and Switzerland appeared under the name NAKOS or NACOS. The reader should bear in mind that Nakos, and other women mentioned in this book, are known to Greek audiences by the slightly different feminine surnames.

2. Michalis Peranthis, *Elliniki Pezografia* [Greek Prose] (Athens: Peranthis, 1968), 4:515.

3. For the best analysis of this period in modern Greek fiction see Thomas Doulis, *Disaster and Fiction* (Berkeley, 1977), especially the chapter entitled "The Generation of the Thirties and Modern Greek Fiction."

4. Personal communication. Rodakis is the author of *Dimosiografia Kai Neoelliniki Pezografia* [Journalism and Modern Greek Prose] (Athens, 1966).

5. Fanis Michalopoulos, "The Modern Greek Novel," *Kathimerini*, April 27, 1936, p. 4.

6. This passage is taken from a third-person account of her life which Nakos wrote for me when I began research for this book. The translation is mine.

7. Nakos spoke to me about her marriage as one of friendship and convenience, and she was characteristically evasive about its dates. Her friends, however, told me that she had married Foskolos only to qualify for the government pension, and that she never lived with him. I was able to determine the dates of her marriage and divorce by much effort and sleuthing in various public records: Nakos was married in 1937 and divorced in 1939. This information lends credence to the friends' version of the story of Nakos's marriage.

8. Some sources, including Nakos herself, say that she had "a slight case" of tuberculosis. Ventiris clearly creates this impression in his introduction to the first edition of *The Deflowered One*, and Nakos's early story "The Bell" portrays a young Greek woman very much like Nakos who is a patient at a sanatarium. However, my inclination is to doubt that she actually contracted the disease. At least one critic, Spyros Melas, was skeptical as well. In a long article hailing Nakos as a rising young writer published in *Ethnos* (June 1928), Melas remarks indulgently, "This Davos! What has she been doing there for so many years: therapy or . . . simply literature with illness?" It is at least possible that she professed illness to explain her residence in Davos, since her relationship with Ventiris was secret. This theory is also supported by a close reading of her story "The Story of the Virginity of Miss Tade," which mentions a young heroine who has blood tests just to make it appear to her father that she has a reason for being in Davos.

9. Not to be confused with the more recent magazine, *Le Monde*.

10. Nakos's friendships with these and other famous Europeans are recounted in her memoir *Personalities I Have Known*.

11. This excerpt, like the one quoted earlier, is from the autobiographical sketch Nakos wrote for me.

12. Yianis Kordatos, *Istoria Tis Neoellinikis Logotechnias* [History of Modern Greek Literature], 2 vols., (Athens, 1962), 2:622.

13. Nakos tells me they are still in Paris, with the "files of Henri Barbusse." I have been trying to locate them.

14. *Great Encyclopaedia of Modern Greek Literature* (Athens: Hari Patsi, 1970), p. 458. The entry was written by Sofia Mavroeidis-Papadakis.
15. Personal communication. She did not have a copy of the alleged manuscript, and she averred that she had never published it.
16. Doulis devotes a chapter to "The Crisis of Greekness" in *Disaster and Fiction*.
17. Doulis's *Disaster and Fiction* concerns the effect of the Asia Minor disaster on modern Greek prose. Numerous books have been written about this historical event, including *The Smyrna Affair* by Marjorie Housepian (New York: Harcourt Brace Jovanovich, 1971).
18. Thomas Doulis, *George Theotokas* (Boston, 1975), p. 86.
19. *The Lost* (Athens, 1970), p. 162. Nakos told me about just such an incident happening to her. Here, as throughout the book, three unspaced dots within a quotation are reproduced exactly as they appear in the original. This is a common form of punctuation in Greek and one Nakos frequently employs to create suspense and heighten impact. Ellipsis will be indicated by three spaced dots.
20. Peter Bien, *Kazantzakis and the Linguistic Revolution in Greek Literature* (Princeton, 1972), p. 224.
21. This and the following quotation are my translation of Nakos' rendition, in Greek, of Uramuno's sentiments, in *Personalities I Have Known* (Athens, 1965).

Chapter Two

1. Nakos kept no record of her publications, and there are no indexes of periodical literature in Greece. Information about earlier Greek and foreign publications is available only at the front and back of Nakos's books, but this information is always incomplete and not verifiable. I located many of Nakos's stories by turning the pages of magazines and newspapers of the late 1920s through World War II. Harry Weinreb located three stories, published in French, in Paris libraries ("Mort du Chrissi," "The Story of the Virginity of Miss Tade," and "Photini"). Five stories were published in small American magazines (1934–41), translated from French by Allan Ross Macdougall ("The Broken Doll," "The Rescue Party," "The House on Fire," "Motherhood," and "The Son"). Three of the stories located in foreign publications ("Mort du Chrissi," "The Fire in the House," and "The Broken Doll") were not available in Greek; the first two were re-translated into Greek for inclusion, along with the other stories I had managed to unearth, in Nakos's collected stories gathered under the title

of one: *I Istoria tis Parthenias tis Despoinidas Tade* [The Story of the Virginity of Miss Tade, Athens, 1981]. No doubt I did not succeed in locating all Nakos's early stories. Furthermore, letters to Swiss, Spanish, and Portuguese libraries have not uncovered stories published in these countries although such publications are referred to in Greek sources.

2. It first appeared in English translation in *Decision* 1, no. 2 (Fall 1941):38–40. From there it was picked up for inclusion in an anthology entitled *Heart of Europe,* ed. Klaus Mann and Hermann Kesten (New York: L. B. Fischer, 1943). From this source it was selected for inclusion in another anthology entitled *A World of Great Stories* ed. Hiram Collins Haydn and John Cournos (New York: Crown, 1947). Finally, the story was found there and reprinted in *Great Short Stories of the World* (Pleasantville, N.Y.: Reader's Digest Association, 1972).

3. "Chance Meeting," published in 1962, is almost exactly the same as "The Lucky One" (1935). The plot is the same, but no two corresponding sentences are identical in wording. My hypothesis is that Nakos translated the story from a French original on two separate occasions. She herself says she has no recollection of the circumstances surrounding either story's writing. That the story was at some point written in French is clear, since Allan Ross Macdougall translated it into English as "The Son," and he did not know Greek.

4. Greek folklore contains many legends of spirits inhabiting wells. Usually the spirit is believed to be "Arapis," that is, a black. See Nicholas Politis, *Laographia* [Folklore] (Athens: Ergani, 1965), p. 250.

5. Page numbers cited in parentheses in the text refer to the collection of stories *The Story of the Virginity of Miss Tade* (Athens, 1981), except for the stories collected as *The Children's Hell* (Athens, 1971), my translations from Greek.

6. This is the same asylum at Daphne which figures in the novel, *The Lost.*

7. Nakos told me that when she was doing translations for the newspaper *Ethnos,* the editor asked her to translate stories written by Nobel prize winners. This seemed to her an impossible request: where would she find such stories? So she wrote them herself, imitating the styles of the authors whose names she put to them. She didn't know what to do, she laughed, when the editor told her that the Italian ambassador was so pleased with a Pirandello story that he wanted to meet the translator to find out where she discovered it! She simply never went to meet him, to the consternation of the editor. I was not able to locate these stories in *Ethnos,* although my inclination is to

Notes and References

believe Nakos's account. At any rate, when I once commented that the story "Fatal Plunge" seemed unlike her usual style, Nakos remarked that perhaps it was one of those she had written as an imitation. (The heroine of *The Deflowered One* performs a similar ploy.)

8. The protagonist is called alternately Antonis and Marios, in one of Nakos's unfortunately not-uncommon lapses into carelessness. Name changes in particular occur in a number of her works, especially *The Deflowered One* and *Mrs. Doremi*.

9. One story, "The Girl From Vietnam," is included in a recent collection, *Ellinides Pezografoi* [Greek Women Prose Writers, 1976]. She has been writing stories again since about 1979, but these are as yet unpublished.

10. *The Children's Inferno* (Hollywood, 1946) is out of print. Unfortunately, the English translation from the French by Allan Ross Macdougall is stilted and literary, hardly reflecting the simple language that is Nakos's hallmark. This can be seen in the title itself, in which Macdougall renders the gut word "hell" as the literary "inferno." I have worked from the Greek edition. Thus, *The Children's Inferno* refers to Macdougall's English translation printed in the United States, and *The Children's Hell* refers to the original Greek, with my translations as needed. Moreover, *The Children's Hell* includes one story, "So That's How Our Life Is," which is not in *The Children's Inferno*.

11. This story is not included in the English edition.

12. This name, which Macdougall translates "Redbreast," actually means "Goldfinch" and is a nickname for the young singer derived from her full name, Katerina. It is a play on the word for "heart."

Chapter Three

1. *The Deflowered One* was reprinted in Greek, in 1937, 1957, and 1980. Page references following quotations refer to the 1937 edition (Pyrsos).

2. Review in *Politeia*, March 27, 1932, p. 5.

3. Quoted in first edition of *The Deflowered One*.

4. "Tade" in Greek means "So-and-so," something like the English "Jane Doe." Nakos uses this same name for the heroine of "The Story of the Virginity of Miss Tade," her first story, and also in her newspaper account of visiting the houses of prostitution in Piraeus, where she introduces herself by that name.

5. The character of Mrs. Kontylo is modelled after Nakos's own nursemaid who bore the same name.

6. *Kokoretsi* is innards grilled on a skewer.
7. Nakos told of hearing about the devil appearing under fig trees from peasant women on the island where she spent summers as a child. Although her mother pooh-poohed the idea, Nakos asserts that she herself experienced just such a vision.
8. Doctors have a special place in this work as in "The Story of the Virginity of Miss Tade," written about the same time. In that story a young woman with the same last name as Katina decides to give up her virginity to the young doctor who has informed her that she has congenital syphilis. It may be relevant, too, that the heroine of *The Lost*, Alexandra, loses her virginity to a doctor, but "scientifically," as she describes it, to please her lover.
9. Kosmas Politis, in *Socialist Life* 4, no. 43 (May 1932):463–64.

Chapter Four

1. *A History of Modern Greek Literature* (Oxford, 1973) p. 260. Several Greek sources published in 1938 and 1939 refer to the imminent publication by Simon and Schuster of an English translation of *The Lost* by Allan Ross Macdougall, but no such publication materialized.
2. *Persons and Texts* (Athens, 1943), *Uneasy Years*, 2:164.
3. The Greek kinship term *theios*, "uncle," is used to refer to a parent's first cousin. Therefore, Sotiris is, in Greek, Alexandra's "Uncle Sotiris."
4. Andreas Karandonis, *Prose Writers and Prose Works of the Generation of '30* (Athens, 1962), p. 229.
5. Page numbers cited in parentheses in the text refer to *The Lost*, my translation from Greek, Estia, 1970.
6. This is not as preposterous as it may seem. The meetings were presumably conducted in Russian, if they were similar to meetings which Nakos tells about in her memoir, *Personalities I Have Known*.
7. Tom Noble pointed out to me the correspondence between the names Nikos/Nakos.
8. One of Nakos's early French stories was entitled "The Fire in the House." Nakos tells me it was published in *Monde,* and the 1955 edition of *Mrs. Doremi* indicates that it was published in Switzerland by Houtsinger Press, in Spanish and Portuguese under the title "Angelica," and in France under the title "Mes Vagabondages" by Denoel. Correspondence with libraries and publishers in France, Switzerland, and Spain has not turned up these publications, but a story entitled "The House on Fire" appears in English translation in *Life and Letters*

7, no. 16. (Spring 1937). In this story, a young boy's fury at his parents leads him to fantasize setting fire to their house, though he ultimately runs away instead. (Since the protagonist of this story is a boy, it seems likely that "Angelica" and "Mes Vagabondages" are different stories.) What is clear is that the notion of setting fire to the family home is an image Nakos found compelling to express seething adolescent emotions.
   9. The grim, ghoulish yet thrilling atmosphere of the Carouge Theater resembles that portrayed in the music hall where the protagonist of Colette's *The Vagabond* performs. It is possible that Nakos was influenced by Colette's novel.
   10. Sister Pagratia is a forerunner of a number of Nakos characters of a similar type. The most fully developed and successful is Victoria in *Toward a New Life*.
   11. Nakos frequently expressed this view to me in conversation, as she did in print in an essay written shortly after her repatriation: "How I View Greek Women," *Ergasia*, Feb. 8, 1930, p. 22.
   12. Apostolis Sahinis, *Prose Writers of Our Time* (Athens, 1967), p. 159.

Chapter Five

   1. Page numbers cited in the text in parentheses refer to *Nafsika*, my translation from Greek, n.p., 1953. (Nakos told me that this book was published by the French Institute in Athens, but no publisher's name appears on the book.)
   2. In her fictionalized biography of Zola serialized in *Akropolis*, Nakos devotes an inordinate amount of attention and space to an event which Zola purportedly witnesses in Marseilles. He becomes involved in the case of a girl who is kept prisoner in the house of a wicked uncle with hypnotic powers. Marseilles seems to have a place in Nakos' imagination as a fitting setting for such sinister and mysterious happenings.
   3. The incident of a child seeing an aborted fetus is used in two other works as well: the early story "The Nameless One" and the novel *Boetian Earth*. See Chapters Two and Seven, respectively, for discussion of these episodes.

Chapter Six

   1. The novel was published in French in book form in 1956 under the title *Madame Do-re-mi, Professeur en Crete* (Paris: Editions Pierre Horay).

2. Page numbers cited in parentheses in the text refer to *Mrs. Doremi*, my translation from Greek, Viper, 1971.
3. Sally has much in common with the character Evel, an American young woman in *Boetian Earth*.

Chapter Seven

1. The official Greek language was not demotic, the spoken idiom, but *katharevousa*, or "puristic," a synthetic formal variety devised as a compromise between the modern spoken language and ancient Greek, to which some wanted to return after the overthrow of Turkish rule. See Bien, *Kazantzakis...*, 1972, for discussion.
2. Lilika Nakos, *Boetian Earth* (Athens, 1964). Hereafter page references from this edition are cited in the text.
3. Doulis, *Theotokas*. See Chapter One for discussion.
4. N. C. Germanacos, "An Interview with Three Contemporary Greek Writers: Stratis Tsirkas, Thanassis Valtinos, George Ioannou," *Boundary 2* 1, no. 2 (Winter 1973):277.
5. Marcel Brion, introduction to *Terre de Béotie* by Lilika Nakos (Lausanne: Société Coopérative Éditions Rencontre, 1962), translated by Yvonne Gauthier.
6. Germanacos, "An Interview," p. 280.
7. The Greek term *levendis* (pl. *levendes*) refers to these old noblemen. The term, however, includes all the positive qualities such as strength, honor, and generosity, which they were reputed to possess. It is interesting to note that guns and books are here equally honored. Lefteris' grandfather in *Mrs. Doremi* makes a similar observation about the connection between guns and books as honorable concerns: "Man should devote himself to arms or letters" (114).

Chapter Eight

1. Michalis Peranthis, *Elliniki Pezografia* [Greek Prose] (Athens: Peranthis, 1968), 4:515.
2. Although clearly it was written many years before its publication in 1960, I have been unable to determine the circumstances in which or exactly when Nakos wrote *Toward a New Life*. She says that she wrote it "after the Occupation," and I believe that this probably means before she left Greece to live in Switzerland in 1947. In January 1953 Nakos wrote a letter to the editor published in the newspaper *Eleftheria* in which she says she has two finished novels that she hasn't been able to publish because in Greece writers must pay to have their work

Notes and References 177

published. I surmise that these were *Boetian Earth* and *Toward a New Life*. Page numbers cited in parentheses in the text refer to *Toward a New Life*, my translation from the Greek (Athens, 1960).

3. The word *ropi,* "tendency," also means "descent" or "decline." This double meaning is appropriate to the interpretation of Barbara's ebb in spirits as a "descent" of sorts.

4. In the novel, as in Nakos's conversation, the character is called *Kyria Viktoria,* "Mrs. Victoria." The use of title-plus-first name is common usage in Greek, reflecting more familiarity than title-plus-surname but more respect than first name alone. This practice is customary in the southern United States as well. However, since this form in English sounds awkward to me, I have omitted the "Mrs." from references to Victoria. I have similarly omitted the title in the cases of characters who are referred to in the novel with title-plus-surname, so that "Mr. Pelopidas" becomes simply "Pelopidas."

5. The dwarf's name, Polyphemos, is the name of the cyclops in *The Odyssey,* associating him with still another legendary monster.

6. In the newspaper *Akropolis,* June 10, 1936, at the beginning of the Metaxas era, there is an article by Lilika Nakos under the headline, "On the Occasion of a Characteristic Situation: HOW THE GOVERNMENT CREATES COMMUNISTS BY FORCE." In this article, Nakos recounts how she applied to the Security Police for permission to go to Russia on a journalistic assignment for *Akropolis* and was turned down because she was considered "dangerous." She repeats a number of times that she has no political affiliations and has never been involved in politics. She therefore berates the government for persecuting innocent citizens in the name of "order" and "security." Using references to the Revolution of 1821 and the grandfathers who died in it, just as she does in *Toward a New Life*, Nakos decries the loss of freedom and warns that it is this very use of force that will drive Greeks to become Communists. She notes, moreover, that many innocent young people are being sent to exile on isolated islands.

The article is written with characteristic Nakos humor and wry charm. For example, Nakos describes her submission of an application to the police chief ("I smile here; I smile there; I smile at the police chief; I even write the application in *Katharevousa* [the formal, official language]") and her conviction that it will be granted without delay, since she is an insignificant "ant," and there is no reason for her to be suspected. When she is told, weeks later, that she is considered "dangerous," she describes her reaction: "Me? 'Dangerous?' All of a sudden I grow taller; I grow larger; I feel myself to be important. I'm flattered."

The earth I'm standing on is shaken. And not to have known it all this time? I descend the stairs with a smile on my lips, so much does a person like flattery! Do you know what 'dangerous' means? That, in other words, the Police are concerned with me. So, you are 'something.' " However, after this initial reaction, Nakos becomes angry: "Not the trip—oh, not the trip at all! But my freedom. Our freedom." Thus the newspaper article offers a glimpse of Nakos's political stance—as well as a testament to her temerity in writing it under the dictatorship.

Chapter Nine

1. After this novel Nakos wrote two memoirs, five fictionalized biographies, and a number of short stories. The memoir *Personalities I Have Known* (Athens: Alvin Redman, 1965; reprinted by Dorikos, 1982) recounts her friendship with famous Europeans: Romain Rolland, Henri Barbusse, Miguel de Unamuno, Albert Einstein, Aldous Huxley, Andre Gide, Colette, Louis-Ferdinand Celine, Simone Weil, and Charles-Ferdinand Ramuz. The other memoir, *Chronicle of a Journalist* (Athens: Dorikos, 1980), tells of her years in journalism and her friendship with prominent Greeks, including the statesman Eleftherios Venizelos. Three of the fictionalized biographies are published as *The Neglected* (Athens: Dorikos, 1978). The others, about Semelweiss and Sister Teresa of Calcutta, are unpublished as yet. The short story "To Koritsi apo to Vietnam" [The Girl from Vietnam] was originally published in an anthology of women's prose and is included in her collected stories (Dorikos, 1981). As yet unpublished is a collection of new stories to be entitled *Oneira kai Afigimata* [Dreams and Stories], which Nakos was still working on when this book went to press.

2. I shall avoid using a name for the archeologist's niece because she has three different names, in a way that Nakos carelessly allows to happen in many of her books. The niece is first called Roza, then is called Eve, and ends up as Marinella.

3. *Ikarian Dreamers* (Athens, 1971), p. 9. Hereafter page references, cited in the text, refer to this edition, my translation from the Greek.

4. *Kallikantzaroi* are mischievous demons which are believed to cause annoying but not dangerous mishaps between Christmas day and Epiphany (January 6). For more information see Stilianos P. Kypriakidou, *Elliniki Laografia* [Greek Folklore], Part I (Athens: Academy of Athens Publications of the Folklore Archive, no. 8 1965), p. 191.

5. "The Catastrophe" is the accustomed Greek term for the Asia Minor disaster. Smyrna is the Greek name for the city now called Izmir

Notes and References

which was inhabited by a large and prosperous Greek population until the 1922 "Catastrophe" forced them to flee. See Chapter One for discussion of this event, as well as Doulis, *Disaster and Fiction*.

6. This scene furnishes an interesting example of how Nakos uses the same themes, techniques, and even incidents in her journalism and in her fiction. The scene in which Kosmas meets Despinio is virtually the same as one in a biography of Peter the Great of Russia that Nakos wrote for *Akropolis*. In that fictionalized biography Peter meets a peasant woman who represents Russia to him just as Despinio represents Ikaria and Greece to Kosmas. In both scenes the women appear mysteriously when the men think themselves totally alone in a forest and yet feel desperately in need. The Russian peasant roams the steppes just as Despinio wanders about the Ikarian villages selling the baskets which her blind father makes. (See *Akropolis*, May 6, 1938, p. 2).

Chapter Ten

1. It has been seen that Nakos's work progressively portrays young children, young women, and women in middle age. One of her stories written in about 1980 and unpublished as this book went to press, entitled "Dorothy", is about the fantasy life of an old woman.

2. Review in *Politeia*, March 27, 1932, p. 5.

Selected Bibliography

PRIMARY SOURCES

1. Books

(The place of publication is Athens, unless otherwise noted.)

Boetian Earth (Gi Tis Voiotiás). Galaxia, 1964. See *Human Fate*.
The Children's Hell (I Kolasi ton Paidion). Estia, 1959; rpt. 1971. Translated into English from French by Allan Ross Macdougall, *The Children's Inferno: Stories of the Great Famine in Greece*, with an introduction by Bessie Breuer. Hollywood: Gateway Books, 1946 (out of print).
Chronicle of a Journalist (To Chroniko Mias Dimosiografos). Dorikos, 1980.
The Deflowered One (I Xepartheni). N.p., 1932; rpt. Pyrsos, 1937; rpt. n.p. 1957; rpt. Dorikos, 1980.
Human Fate (Anthropina Pepromena). Vivlioekdotiki, 1955; rpt. as *Boetian Earth*, 1964; rpt. as *Human Fate*, Dorikos, 1978.
Ikarian Dreamers (Oramatistes tis Ikarias). Fexis, 1963; rpt. Papyros Press (Viper), 1971; rpt. Dorikos, 1982.
The Life of Edgar Poe (I Zoi tou Edgar Poe). Estia, 1936. See *Nevermore*.
The Lost (Oi Parastratimenoi). Estia, 1970. (5 earlier editions out of print).
Mrs. Doremi (I Kyria Doremi). Difros, 1955; rpt. Papyros Press (Viper), 1971; rpt. Dorikos, 1981.
Nafsika. N.p., 1953; rpt. Dorikos, 1980 under the cover of *The Deflowered One*.
The Neglected (Oi Paragnorismenoi). Dorikos, 1978.
Nevermore (Pote Pia). Papyros Press (Viper), 1975 (rpt. of *The Life of Edgar Poe*, Estia, 1936); rpt. Dorikos, 1981.
Personalities I Have Known (Prosopikotites Pou Gnorisa). Alvin Redman, 1965; rpt. Dorikos, 1982.

The Story of the Virginity of Miss Tade (I Istoria tis Parthenias tis Despoinidas Tade). Dorikos, 1981. Collected short stories.
Toward a New Life (Yia Mia Kainouryia Zoi). Mavroyiorgi, 1960; rpt. Dorikos, 1976.

2. Stories

Except for "The Broken Doll" the following stories are collected in *The Story of The Virginity of Miss Tade,* Dorikos, 1981.

"... And the Child Lied..." (... *Kai to Paidi Eipe Psemata* ...). Included in first edition of *The Deflowered One.*
"The Bastard" *(O Nothos).* Ergasia 1, no. 15 (1930): 23–24.
"The Bell" *(To Koudouni).* Included in first edition of *The Deflowered One.*
"The Bond" *(O Desmos).* Tomes 48 (1979): 20–23. Translated from Greek into English by Deborah Tannen as, "Lilika Nakos Writes About her Mother," Women's Studies 6, no. 3 (1978): 218–22.
"The Broken Doll." Translated into English from French by Allan Ross Macdougall. Life and Letters 15, no. 6 (1936): 96–98.
"Chance Meeting" *(Tychaia Synandisi).* Filologiki Protochronia 19 (1962): 27–20. (A rewriting of "The Lucky One" [*To Tychero*], Nea Estia 18, no. 216 (1935): 42–46. Translated into English by Allan Ross Macdougall as "The Son," Story 9, no. 49 (1936): 95–100.
"Fatal Plunge" *(Thanasimi Voutia).* Filologiki Protochronia 18 (1961): 151–54.
"The Father" *(O Pateras).* Neoelliniki Grammata, Jan. 2, 1937, p. 3. Translated into English from French by Allan Ross Macdougall as "The Rescue Party," Lovat Dickson's Magazine 3, no. 4 (1934): 457–62.
"The Girl From Vietnam" *(To Koritsi apo to Vietnam).* Greek Women Prose Writers *(Ellinides Pezografoi),* edited by Ersi Lange. Athens: Synchroni Epochi, 1975, pp. 191–95.
"The House on Fire" *(Fotia Sto Spiti).* Translated into English from French by Allan Ross Macdougall, Life and Letters 16, no. 7 (1937): 54–56. Re-translated into Greek for inclusion in *The Story of the Virginity of Miss Tade.* Athens: Dorikos, 1981.
"The Little Servant" *(To Doulaki).* Neoelliniki Logotechnia 2, no. 2 (1939): 36–42; rpt. *Journalism and Modern Greek Prose (Dimosiografia Kai Neoelliniki Pezografia),* edited by Pericles Rodakis. Athens: Diana, 1966, pp. 676–81.

"Love" *(Agapi)*. Nea Estia 14, no. 161 (1933): 910–12.
"Mort du Chrissi" (Chrysa's Death). Bifur 2 (1928): 16–23. Translated from French into Greek by Nakos for inclusion in collected stories as *O Thanatos tis Chrysas*.
"Motherhood" *(Mitrotis)*. O Kyklos 4 (1934): 116–18. "Maternity," translated into English from French by Allan Ross Macdougall, *Decision* 1, no. 2 (1941): 38–40. Repeatedly anthologized in English.
"Murky Story" *(Tholi Istoria)*. Nea Estia 15, no. 172 (1934): 164–66.
"The Nameless One" *(O Akatanomastos)*. Included in first edition of *The Deflowered One*.
"Photini" *(Foteini)*. Nouvelles Litteraires, Jan. 1928; translated from French into Greek by Galateia Kazantzakis, *I Proia*, Feb. 4, 1928, p. 3.
"Spring Invitation" *(Anoixiatiko Kalesma)*. Nea Estia 15, no. 176 (1934): 347–49.
"The Story of the Virginity of Miss Tade" *(I Istoria tis Parthenias Tis Despoinidas Tade)*. Included in first edition of *The Deflowered One*. "Histoire de la Virginité de la Demoiselle Une Telle," Europe 16 (1928): 175–78.

3. Serialized Fictionalized Biographies

(Unless otherwise noted, from *Akropolis*)

Apollonios, The Tyanean, the Great Wizard of Antiquity. Feb. 7, 1937 through Mar. 13, 1937 (36 segs.).
The Earthshaking Life of Leo Tolstoy. Oct. 22, 1940 through Dec. 31, 1940. (Segments sporadic because of World War II).
Edison, the Great Wizard of the Twentieth Century. May 30, 1937 through Aug. 7, 1937 (70 segs.).
Erasmia Bertsa. Nea Estia, 98, no. 1159 through 98, no. 1162 (1975). (4 segs.).
The Fantastic Adventures of the Renowned Explorer Marco Polo in China. Dec. 5, 1937 through Jan. 3, 1938 (28 segs.).
George Sand and her Famous Love Affairs with the Greatest Men of Her Time. Nov. 1, 1936 through Nov. 29, 1936 (29 segs.).
The Heroic Life of George Washington. May 14, 1939 through June 16, 1939 (34 segs.).
The Heroic Life of Pasteur, the Man who Saved and Saves Human Lives by the Thousands. Aug. 8, 1937 through Dec. 20, 1937 (134 segs.).

Jean-Jacques Rousseau: The Astonishing Man and his Adventurous Life. Jan. 29, 1939 through Mar. 13, 1939 (43 segs.).

The Legendary Love of the Wise Theologian Abelard and his Beautiful Student Heloise. Oct. 1, 1936 through Oct. 30, 1936 (30 segs.).

The Life and Loves of the Great Dramatic Actress Eleonora Duse with the Poet Gabriel d'Annunzio. Aug. 9, 1936 through Oct. 2, 1936 (54 segs.).

The Life and Loves of the Immortal Moliere. Jan. 3, 1937 through Feb. 7, 1937 (36 segs.); rpt. *Ora,* Sept. 1956 (22 segs.).

The Life of Ehrlich. Mar. 16, 1941 through Apr. 24, 1941 (22 segs.).

The Life, Prophecy and Magic of Nostradamos. Mar. 21, 1937 through May 30, 1937 (69 segs.).

The Man Who Triumphed Over His Fate: Franklin Roosevelt. Aug. 8, 1940 through Sept. 2, 1940 (24 segs.).

Marquess Pompadour, the Renowned Favorite of King Louis XV. Dec. 1, 1936 through Dec. 30, 1936 (30 segs.).

The Masterpiece by Mistral: Mireille, rewritten as a novel. *Embros.* Nov. 10, 1946 through Dec. 11, 1946 (30 segs.).

Moscho Tzavella. O Asyrmatos. June 12, 1939 through June 22, 1939 (12 segs.).

Peter the Great, the Creator of Russia. Apr. 1, 1938 through July 24, 1938 (118 segs.).

The Tragic Life of Emile Zola. Dec. 28, 1937 through Mar. 27, 1938 (88 segs.).

The Tragic Life of Feodor Dostoevsky, the Comforter of the Humble and the Scorned. Sept. 25, 1939 through Nov. 12, 1938 (48 segs.).

The Tragic Life of the Swedish Sage Alfred Nobel. June 16, 1940 through Aug. 3, 1940 (47 segs.).

SECONDARY SOURCES

Bien, Peter. *Kazantzakis and the Linguistic Revolution in Greek Literature.* Princeton: Princeton University Press, 1972. Bien's analysis of the language question in Greece and its relation to the modern Greek novel is invaluable for an understanding of the issues and trends crucial to the work of Nakos and the other writers of her generation.

Diktaios, Ari. *Anazitites Prosopou* [Investigators of the Person]. Athens: Fexis, 1963, pp. 117–19. Originally written in 1953, the section on Nakos is a reasonable if not inspired introduction to her work until then.

Dimaras, Constantine. *A History of Modern Greek Literature.* Translated by Mary Gianos. London: University of London Press, 1969. An introduction to modern Greek literature.

———. "A Sure Talent." Review of *The Deflowered One. Politeia,* March 27, 1932, p. 5. An analysis of Nakos's first major publication in Greek and its significance for the modern Greek novel.

Doulis, Thomas. *Disaster and Fiction.* Berkeley: University of California Press, 1977. A study of the impact of the Asia Minor disaster on the modern Greek novel and the group of writers called The Generation of the Thirties. Among the best work that has been done on modern Greek prose.

———. *George Theotokas.* Boston: Twayne Publishers, 1975. Twayne World Authors Series #339. This excellent study of the novelist of the same generation contains many insights helpful to an understanding of Nakos's work.

Germanacos, N. C. "An Interview with Three Contemporary Greek Writers: Stratis Tsirkas, Thanassis Valtinos, George Ioannou." *Boundary 2* 1, no. 2 (1973): 270–313. An excellent discussion of the conditions and problems related to writing prose in Greek, past and present, by those who are in the best position to know.

Ieronymidis, Loula. *Lilika Nakou: Anaskopisi sto Ergo tis kai Polla Keimena Dika tis* [Lilika Nakos: A Review of Her Work with Many Excerpts]. Athens: Kritikon Fyllon, 1974. A sketchy introduction to Nakos's life and work. Confusing to read since direct and indirect quotations are mixed in and not marked.

Karandonis, Andreas. *Pezografoi kai Pezografia tis Yenias tou '30* [Prose Writers and Prose Works of the Generation of '30]. Athens: Fexis, 1962. Originally printed in *Ta Nea Grammata* in 1936, the article on Nakos focuses on her novel *The Lost* in rather general terms.

Kordatos, Yianis. *Istoria tis Neoellinikis Logotechnias* [History of Modern Greek Literature from 1453 to 1961]. 2 Vols. Athens: Vivlioekdotiki, 1962. An introduction to modern Greek literature. Vol. 2 discusses Nakos's contribution (pp. 638–40).

Melas, Spyros ["Fortounio"]. "About a Greek Woman Writer." *Ethnos,* June 9, 1928. This article introduced Nakos to Greek audiences, commenting on her life and work in Paris.

Michalopoulos, Fanis. "The Greek Novel: Lilika Nakos." *Kathimerini,* April 27, 1936, p. 4. After a brief introduction to the Greek novel up to that time, focuses on Nakos as one of the most important

new novelists. Makes the mistake of calling her fiction "autobiography," but has valid observations nonetheless.
NEOELLINIKA GRAMMATA. "Lilika Nakos." Jan. 8, 1938, pp. 12–15. A portrait of Nakos, including her views on writing and her own life.
Panayiotopoulos, I. M. *Ta Prosopa Kai Ta Keimena* [Persons and Texts]. Athens: Aetos, 1943. Vol. 2, *Uneasy Years: Modern Greek Prose between the Wars.* The volume contains an introduction to the literature of the period. The section on Nakos (pp. 158–167) contains some critical and much biographical information, not all correct.
Politis, Kosmas. Review of *The Deflowered One. Sosialistiki Zoi* [Socialist Life] 4, no. 43 (1932): 463–64. Interprets the book from a political perspective yet includes interesting comments on Nakos's style.
Politis, Linos. *A History of Modern Greek Literature.* Oxford: Oxford University Press, 1973. An introduction to modern Greek literature. Nakos is one of only two women of the Generation of the Thirties mentioned. (The other is Melpo Axioti.)
Rodakis, Pericles. *Dimosiografia Kai Neoelliniki Pezografia* [Journalism and Modern Greek Prose]. Athens: Diana, 1966. Includes a particularly insightful introduction to modern Greek prose, by period, discussed in light of political and social forces, followed by examples, including one of Nakos's best stories. Rodakis educated himself while he spent almost all his adult life as a political prisoner.
Sahinis, Apostolis. *Pezografoi tou Kairou Mas* [Prose Writers of Our Time]. Athens: Estia, 1967. Nakos is one of seventeen writers discussed (pp. 157–65); the only other woman is Galateia Kazantzakis. Evidences minimal critical acumen.
Tannen, Deborah. "Lilika Nakos and Other Greek Women Prosewriters." *Pilgrimage* 2, no. 5 (May 1976). Traces Nakos's views of women in her work.
―――. "Coming of Age in the Modern Greek Novels of Lilika Nakos." *Regionalism and the Female Imagination* 4, no. 1 (Spring 1978). Traces the theme of coming of age and sexuality in Nakos's work.
―――. "Mothers and Daughters in the Modern Greek Novels of Lilika Nakos." *Women's Studies* 6, no. 3 (Fall 1978): 205–15. Traces the development of relationships between mothers and daughters in Nakos's work. Appears together with a memoir of her mother by Nakos, translated by Deborah Tannen, and numerous photographs.
"What do Writers Like Best?" *Nea Estia,* 845 (Sept. 15, 1962), p. 1349. Nakos comments on her work, stating her preference for

the collection of stories *The Children's Hell* because of its social impact.

Yiofillis, Fotos. "Our Post-War Prose." *Asyrmatos,* June 25, 1939, pp. 3–5. Focuses on Nakos and another woman, Irene Athinaia. Effective view of her personality and her own observations about her work, Greek literature, and journalism.

Index

Abortion, 31, 83, 87, 111–12, 116
Adolescence, 66–67, 112–14
Akropolis, 7, 15, 35, 59; *See also,* Journalism
Alexiou, Elli, 5, 11, 17
America, 154
Androgyny, 72, 86–87, 117–18, 137–39
Art, 107
Asia Minor, 12, 153
Asia Minor Disaster, 19, 26–27, 153–54, 171n17, 178n5
Athens, 24; *See also The Lost, Toward a New Life, The Children's Hell*
Atomic bomb, 24, 145, 149
Avyeris, Markos, 5

Barbusse, Henri, 5
Bien, Peter, 20–21, 24
Bildungsroman, 59
Bouboulina, 139
Brion, Marcel, 123
Bronte, Emily, *Wuthering Heights,* 81

Characterization in novels, 159–61, 163; idealized, 53, 56, 86–89, 123, 160

Children, 25, 28–32; *See also* Nakos, Short Stories, & *The Children's Hell*
Christ, 14, 78, 79, 81
Christian symbolism, 50–52, 98, 139–40, 152
Civil War, 9, 93
Communism, 57–58, 63, 119–20, 126–27, 139–42, 151, 177n6
Crete, 24, 93–103

Davos, Switzerland, 5, 14, 17, 31–32
Dickinson, Emily, 97
Dimaras, Constantine, 4, 45, 166
Divorce, 88
Doctors, 53–54, 90, 174n8
Doulis, Thomas, 20, 123

Einstein, Albert, 5
Emotion, 34, 48, 59, 96, 113
Escapism, 17, 96, 110–11, 121–22, 131–32
Ethnos, 6
Expatriation, 16, 20, 32, 48, 61, 103, 122, 154

Family, Greek, 120

187

Fathers, 15, 29, 34, 47–48, 54–56, 75–77, 93–94, 99–100; See also Nakos, Loukas
Folklore & Mythology, ancient Greek, 84–86
  Demeter, 139
  Dionysus, 152, 157
  Icarus, 152
  Mt. Parnassus, 109, 110
  Muses, 109–110
  Satyr, 67
Folklore, modern Greek
  Devil under fig tree, 31, 174n7
  Spirit in well, 28, 53, 172n4
Forgiveness, 42–43, 143
Foskolos, Constantine, 5, 9
Freedom, 99–100, 120–22, 141–42, 143
Freudian interpretation, 30, 53–55, 75

Generation of the Thirties, 3, 11, 19–20, 56
Geneva, Switzerland, 16, 18, 20, 21, 24, 59; See also *The Lost*
German Occupation, 8–9, 20–21, 25, 36–44, 81, 93, 104, 123–25; See also *The Children's Hell*
Germanacos, N.C., 123
Gide, Andre, 5
God, 39–40, 41, 42, 152–53
Greece, Image of, 48, 58, 92, 93
Greek-Americans, 10, 16, 23, 107, 145, 156; See also *Ikarian Dreamers*

Greekness, 17, *18–21*, 22–24, 123–25, 142–43, 152–54

Hellenism, 123–25

Ikaria, 10, 18, 22, 144, 152–54; See also *Ikarian Dreamers*
Innocence, 30, 39–41, 59, 63–64
Isolation, 16, 21–22, 25, 27–28, 77–79, 96, 121, 132

Journalism, 1, 6–11, 13–15, 27, 130, 177n6, 179n6
Joyce, James, 20

Karelli, Zoe, 12
Kazantzakis, Galateia, 5, 11, 12, 25
Kazantzakis, Nikos, 5, 12, 14, 20–21, 24
Kordatos, Yianis, 12

Language, Greek, 22, 23–24
  Demotic, 3, 14, 59, 134, 163
  Katharevousa, 3, 165
Language question, The, 3, 12, 176n1
Loneliness, 16, 21–22, 25, 28, 71–72, 77–79, 86
Love, 16, 22, 26, 29, 32–34, 37–39, 60, 62, 66–69, 70–72, 72–77, 77–78, 89–90, 96, 102, 113–14, 116, 135–37, 157–58

Macdougall, Allan Ross, 25
Macedonia, 41

Index

Marriage, 16, 34, 47, 87, 89–90, 100, 102, 114–16, 131, 137, 161, 165
Marseilles, 16, 24, 26, 29, 86, 175n2; *See also* Nafsika
Melissanthi, 1
Men, 68, 70–72
   Characterization of, 136–37
   Greek, 79
   Masculinity, 42
Menstruation, 66, 112–13, 118
Metaxas dictatorship, 7, 24, 126–28, 132, 140; *See also* Toward a New Life
Midwives, 86–87
Molestation, 30, 54–55, 67–68
Money, 88, 116, 156
Mothers, 29, 30–31, 56–57, 66, 75–76, 80–81, 84–85, 137–38; *See also* Papadopoulos, Eleni
Motherhood, 49, 51–53
Music, 64, 82–83, 85–86, 96, 102, 109, 110
Myrtiotissa, 12

Nakos, Lilika
   Birthdate, 169n1
   Father; *See* Nakos, Loukas
   Marriage, 170n7
   Mother; *See* Papadopoulos, Eleni
   Musician, 17
   Political orientation, 17–18, 63
   Teacher, 13, 59, 126
   Works, Fictionalized Biographies, 11, 15, 24
   Works, in French, 5, 9, 16, 22, 23–24, 25, 26, 29, 31, 36, 45, 59, 80, 175n1

WORKS, MEMOIRS, 178n1
Chronicle of a Journalist, 7
Personalities I Have Known, 5, 11, 18

WORKS, NOVELS, 24
Boetian Earth, 9, 16, 21, 24, 81, 83, 104–125, 127, 129, 135
Deflowered One, The, 3, 6, 14, 15, 16, 24, 25, 30, 45–58, 74, 80, 81, 83, 84, 86, 89, 93, 102, 166
Human Fate; See Boetian Earth
Ikarian Dreamers, 10, 16, 21, 23, 24, 81, *144–63*
Lost, The, 16, 18, 20, 24, 30, 32, 36, 59–79, 80, 81, 82, 83, 86, 89, 95, 102, 130, 131
Mrs. Doremi, 6, 9, 24, 83, 93–103
Nafsika, 12, 16, 24, 29, 80–92, 100, 131
Toward a New Life, 6, 7, 16, 24, 81, 104, *126–44*, 166, 176n2

WORKS, SHORT STORIES, 16, 24, *25–44*, 81, 171n1, 172n2,3,7, 173n10, 174n8, 179n1
"And the Child Lied," 29–30
"Air Raid," 42
"Bastard, The," 29
"Bell, The," 32

"Broken Doll, The," 29
"Buddies," 37, 38
"Cat, The," 37, 38–39
Children's Hell, The, 8, 9, 16, 21, 24, 25, 36–44, 80, 104
"Chrysa's Death," 29, 60
"Elenitsa," 40–41
"Englishman, The," 37–38
"Eye of God, The," 40
"Fatal Plunge," 34
"Father, The," 34
"Giovanni," 37, 38
"God's Garden," 39–40, 43–44
"Grandmother's Sin, The," 42
"House on Fire, The," 30
"Immortal Race," 43
"Karderina," 39, 43
"Little Servant, The," 27–28
"Love," 6, 32–33, 34
"Love," in *The Children's Hell,* 37, 43–44
"Lucky One, The," 27
"Macedonia," 41
"Madwoman, The," 40
"Maternity," 26–27, 30
"Murky Story, A," 35
"Nameless One, The," 30–31, 111, 113
"Photini," 5, 12, 25, 28
"So That's How Our Life Is," 37, 39
"Son, The"; *See* "The Lucky One"
"Spring Invitation," 6, 32, 33–34
"Story of the Virginity of Miss Tade, The," 31–32

Nakos, Loukas, 3, 12, 14, 17, 21, 78, 166; *See also* Fathers
Nature, 82, 153
Naturalism, 15
Nea Estia, 6
New York, 155
Novel, The Greek, 45
Nuns, 71, 108
Nursemaids, 51, 52–53, 84–85, 90, 173n5

Occult; *See* Spiritualism
Odyssey (Homer), 84–85

Palamas, Kostis, 45
Panayiotopoulos, I.M., 59
Papadakis, Sofia, 5
Papadopoulos, Arsenoe, 12
Papadopoulos, Eleni, 3, 9, 12, 21, 22, 93, 166; *See also* Mothers
Papanastassiou, Alexander, 17
Parental love, 74–77
Parents, alienation from, 15, 22, 29, 30, 103; *See also* Fathers & Mothers
Peasants, 52–53
Poe, Edgar Allan, 35
Point of view, 33, 35, 37, 43–44, 60, 63–64, 73, 92, 98, 104, 133–35, 145, 148–49
Political oppression, 140–43, 177n6
Politics, 107, 114, 150–51
Politis, Kosmas, 56
Politis, Linos, 59
Polydouri, Maria, 12

Revolution of 1821, 124–25, 139

Index

Rodakis, Pericles, 3, 185
Rolland, Romain, 4

Sartre, Jean-Paul, 14
Schools, 125
Sexuality, 3, 28, 29–32, 45, 54–55, 63–64, 65–69, 111–14, 135–37, 146, 157–58, 165
Siblings, 29, 37, 43–44, 60, 64–65
Sikelianos, 142
Social class, 15, 17–18, 21, 28, 29, 55, 57, 98, 130–31, 133, 166
Social criticism, 15, 26–28, 44, 56–58, 59–60, 69–70, 90–92, 98–99, 119–20, 151
Social novel, 3, 15, 163
Spiritualism, 14–15, 35, 81, 84–86, 107–109, 153
Stavrou, Tatiana, 11–12
Structure of works, 26–27, 48–49, 61–62, 78–79, 82–83, 96–97, 163
Style of works, 3, 14, 59–60, 92, 103, 104, 133–35, 149, 156, 166; present tense, 64, 78
Suicide, 28, 78
Syphilis, 32, 48–49

Themes in works, 14, 15–24, 149, 164–65

Theotokas, George, 123
Theotokis, Constantine, 5
Tsirkas, Stratis, 123
Tuberculosis, 32, 62, 97, 170n8

Unamuno, Miguel de, 5, 23–24

Varnalis, Kostas, 5, 20
Venizelos, Eleftherios, 17; See also *Chronicle of a Journalist*
Ventiris, George, 4, 5, 6, 14, 17–18, 22, 48–49, 78
Village vs. city, 27–28, 94, 98, 101, 107

Weil, Simone, 5
Women
  Characterization of, 71–72, 86–88, 100, 101–102, 128–29, 136–40, 145, 160–62
  Greek, 78–79
  Men's attitude toward, 66, 72, 102, 118–19, 165
  Names of Greek, 169
  Victimization of, 27, 56–57, 69, 89, 90–92, 116–19
  Working, 6, 8, 13, 15–16, 90, 94, 117
Writers, 3, 11–13, 15–16, 22, 163
World War II, 80, 93, 131, 150

Yogananda, *The Autobiography of a Yogi*, 14, 81